Spirits & Cocktails

· OF ·

UPSTATE

NEW YORK

Spirits & Cocktails
· OF ·
UPSTATE
NEW YORK

A History

DON CAZENTRE

AMERICAN PALATE

Published by American Palate
A Division of The History Press
Charleston, SC
www.historypress.net

Copyright © 2017 by Don Cazentre
All rights reserved

First published 2017

Manufactured in the United States

ISBN 9781467137003

Library of Congress Control Number: 2017945030

CONTENTS

Contents

ACKNOWLEDGEMENTS

Over the last decade or so, I've collected and read lots of books on the topic of mixed drinks. They include *The Joy of Mixology* by Gary Regan, *Vintage Spirits and Forgotten Cocktails* by Ted Haigh and *Imbibe!* by David Wondrich, not to mention old reprints like *The Stork Club Bar Book*, *The Old Waldorf-Astoria Bar Book* and the one that started it all: *How to Mix Drinks*, written by Jerry Thomas in 1862.

It seems I was destined to write my own book on the history and culture of spirits and cocktails. Needless to say, the drinks authors cited above, and others, provided an invaluable resource. They proved that drinking is a suitable topic for a book. If you're interested in drinks and their stories, you need to read their work.

Once I started, it took more than a year—and lots of help—to complete this book.

A big thank-you goes to those in the Upstate drinks industry who took the time to meet and welcome me to their distilleries, bars and shops for interviews. Special mention goes to Jori Jayne Emde at Fish & Game in Hudson, Ralph Erenzo at Tuthilltown Spirits in Gardiner, Jason "Jay" Bowers at Excelsior Pub in Albany, Doug Plummer at the American Hotel in Sharon Springs, Joe Fee at Fee Brothers in Rochester, Jason Barrett at Black Button Distilling in Rochester, Brian McKenzie at Finger Lakes Distilling near Watkins Glen, Joe Myer at Myer Farm Distillers in Seneca County, Chris Uyehara at Last Shot Distilling in Skaneateles, the Carvell brothers at Old Home Distillers in Lebanon, Mike Aubertine at Clayton Distilling in the Thousand Islands, Ben Reilley at Life of Reilley Distilling and the beverage and nightlife crew at Turning Stone Resort Casino in Verona. Also thanks to Eva Nicklas and Kathryn Serriani of the Lewiston Council on the Arts, Natalie Stetson at the Erie Canal Museum and Jeremy Hammill of the Scotch 'n Sirloin in DeWitt.

As a longtime journalist, I had little direct experience with historical research. For help with that, I'm indebted to Kihm Winship and his work on Skaneateles history, Dennis Connors of the Onondaga Historical Association in Syracuse and Craig Gravina of the New York State Museum in Albany, who pointed me to the records of the archaeological dig at the Quackenbush Still House site.

Thanks to Amanda Irle, my contact at The History Press, for her guidance and patience. To my sister, Julie Cazentre, much appreciation for the support and the place to crash when in the Albany area.

And as always, to my wife, Maureen Fitzsimmons, thanks for everything.

INTRODUCTION

To some extent, Upstate New York exists in the giant shadow cast by one of the world's greatest cities. No one would argue about New York City's place in history, certainly not in the history of a subject as universal and sophisticated as spirits and cocktails.

And yet Upstate New York, from the Hudson Valley to the Niagara River, has its own long and grand connection to the history of drinks and drinking in America.

Colonial-era rum was distilled here. The first recorded definition of the word *cocktail* was printed here. Whiskey floated down the Erie Canal here. The most celebrated bartender of the golden age of the cocktail was born here. Along with history, there are plenty of stories—myths and lore, some fiction. They involve rooster's feathers, angels seeking their wings and more.

But it's not just about old stories. Upstate New York today is the home of a resurgent cocktail culture, fueled by more than one hundred modern distillers and beverage makers, countless bars and untold numbers of drinks enthusiasts. They complete the tale.

No book this size can tell the complete story of a region so big, a history so long and a contemporary drinking culture so diverse. Consider it a guide to some of the best stories, old and new. For the most part, they're told in chronological (historical) order. Every so often, however, there's a detour to a modern place or person that complements the history. And there are cocktail recipes—more than sixty of them—from historic classics to current creative concoctions.

Grab a drink, and let's begin.

1

UPSTATE NEW YORK AND
THE ORIGINS OF THE COCKTAIL

History, Stories, Legends

On May 13, 1806, the editor of a newspaper serving Hudson, New York, responded to a query from a reader. The reader had encountered the phrase "cock tail" in the previous week's edition and wondered what it meant.

"Cock tail, then," the editor wrote, "is a stimulating liquor, composed of spirits of any kind, sugar, water and bitters."

That answer established an enduring link between Upstate New York and that great American invention, the cocktail.

It may not have been the first known use of "cock tail" or "cocktail" in print, though it certainly seems to be an early one. It does appear to be the first time in recorded history that the word was accompanied by a definition of a certain type of mixed alcoholic drink.

In 1806, Hudson was a prosperous whaling and merchant town on the Hudson River south of Albany. There seems to be no specific reason why it should be a cradle of the cocktail. But Hudson isn't the only Upstate locale with a claim to cocktail history.

Folks in Lewiston, on the Niagara River near Niagara Falls in western New York, contend that their town is the place where, for the first time, a tavern keeper placed a rooster's feather in a drink and called it a "cock tail."

A place called the Four Corners in Westchester County (near the current town of Elmsford) has a related claim. In his Revolutionary War novel *The*

Above: Masthead of the *Balance & Columbian Repository*, Hudson, New York, which printed the first definition of the word "cocktail" in 1806. *Courtesy of Ted Haigh.*

Right: James Fenimore Cooper, author of *The Spy*. *New York Public Library.*

JAMES F. COOPER.

Spy, author James Fenimore Cooper assigns the birth of the feathery drink called the cocktail to a woman running a tavern in Four Corners. That may have been the first recorded use of the word *cocktail* in fiction. It turns out that Cooper, a native Upstate New Yorker, once spent some time in Lewiston, where he may have first heard (or even witnessed) the cocktail story.

The actual origin of the cocktail—the word and the drink—is steeped in mystery, speculation and outright fantasy. "The word 'cocktail' itself remains one of the most elusive in the language," William Grimes wrote in his 2001 book, *Straight Up or On the Rocks: The Story of the American Cocktail.*

In 1946, the writer H.L. Mencken, who had made up a number of specious cocktail stories of his own, compiled a book called *American English.* Among the many words and phrases he tried to track down was "cocktail." He found at least forty different origin stories, or etymologies. "Nearly all of them," he wrote, "are no more than baloney."

In recent years, no one has done more to track down the origins of the cocktail and sort out the baloney than author and drinks historian David Wondrich. His works include *Imbibe!*, a history that traces the cocktail primarily through the life and work of celebrated nineteenth-century mixologist Jerry Thomas (who, it should be noted, was born in the Upstate New York town of Sackets Harbor on the shore of Lake Ontario).

"Every single one of the drink's early mentions fits neatly into the triangle between New York (City), Albany, and Boston," Wondrich wrote in an appendix to *Imbibe!*, published in 2007. "If we follow the available evidence, then the Cocktail originated somewhere in the Hudson Valley, Connecticut or western Massachusetts."

In a 2016 article for *Saveur* magazine, titled "Ancient Mystery Revealed! The Real History (Maybe) of How the Cocktail Got Its Name," Wondrich re-examined that conclusion. He admits to "poking around" Lewiston for answers. He also traces the links between that story and Cooper's fictional account in Westchester County.

"The history of the cocktail—and here I mean the original cocktail, the ur-mixture of spirits, bitters, sugar, and water that spawned the whole enticing tribe—has (perhaps not surprisingly) always been like this: heady with false leads and spiked with treacherous maybes," Wondrich concludes.

Yet that Upstate New York connection persists. The river town of Hudson. Lewiston on the Niagara. Westchester County. Plot those places on a map and you get a triangle that neatly fits the place we call Upstate.

Maybe—just maybe—the cocktail was born in Upstate New York.

WHAT IS A COCKTAIL, ANYWAY?

Today, the cocktail encompasses a whole array of mixed alcoholic beverages. Back in the early 1800s, there were already other several identifiable types of mixed drinks. Punch was a popular type, as were the sangaree, the julep, the nog, the toddy, the cobbler, the shrub and others.

So was a concoction called a sling. The Hudson newspaper account, after dispensing the aforementioned definition of cocktail, says it is "vulgarly called a bittered sling." The sling—spirits, sugar and water without the bitters—was already a known item. In any case, once the name "cocktail" took hold, it veered away from the original definition. Notably, while some latter-day cocktails still contain bitters, many do not.

"Americans still drink all sorts of things before, during and after a meal and would probably call every one of them a cocktail if it was cold and had some spirit as a base," Grimes writes in *Straight Up or On the Rocks*. "'Cocktail and 'mixed drink' have often become synonymous," he notes, although the cocktail has even grown to include single-ingredient drinks.

"Common sense and custom suggest that a cocktail should be cold and snappy," he continues. "It should be invigorating to the palate and pleasing to the eye. That covers most of the territory." That's how martinis and Manhattans, margaritas and mai tais, not to mention all sorts of highballs, shots and more come to be known today as cocktails.

But did cocktails get their start in Upstate New York?

The Case for Hudson

In the 2016 article for *Saveur*, Wondrich describes the early newspaper reference in Hudson as "well worn." By that he means it's appeared in almost every cocktail book written in the past century. The key passages show up in two consecutive issues of the newspaper, which went by the name *Balance & Columbian Repository*, on May 6 and May 13, 1806.

The newspaper, like many in those days, was partisan in its politics. The *Balance* was firmly in the camp of the Federalist Party (George Washington, Alexander Hamilton and so on) and was in favor of a strong national government. It opposed the Democrats (Thomas Jefferson, among others) who stood for decentralized government. In 1806, Jefferson was president. The *Balance* introduced the word "cock-tail" on May 6, when it took a swipe at a Democratic candidate for state legislature in nearby Claverack, New York. That Democrat apparently had "used up the town's stocks of alcohol in a frenzy of boozy vote-buying." The article went on to list the candidate's tab as covering "720 rum-grogs, 17 dozen brandies, 32 gin-slings, 411 glasses of bitters and 25 dozen 'cock-tails.'"

The next week, the historic cocktail definition appears in what is essentially the letters to the editor section. The reader's query, written in that wonderfully archaic early American style, was in response to the article on the candidate in Claverack:

> *Sir, I observe in your paper of the 6th inst. in the account of a democratic candidate for a seat in the Legislature, marked under the head of Loss, 25*

do., "cock tail." Will you be so obliging as to inform me what is meant by this species of refreshment?…I have heard of a "jorum" of "phlegm cutter" and "fog driver," of "wetting the whistle" and "moistening the clay," of a "fillip," a "spur in the head," "quenching a spark in the throat," of "flip," etc., but never in my life, though I have lived a good many years, did I hear of a cock tail before. Is it peculiar to this part of the country? Or is it a late invention? Is the name expressive of the effect which the drink has on a particular part of the body? Or does it signify that the Democrats who make the potion are turned topsy-turvy, and have their heads where their tails are?

The editor, Harry Croswell, responded:

As I make it a point, never to publish any thing (under my editorial head) but what I can explain, I shall not hesitate to gratify the curiousity of my inquisitive correspondent—Cock tail, then, is a stimulating liquor, composed of spirits of any kind, sugar, water, and bitters—it is vulgarly called a bittered sling and supposed to be an excellent electioneering potion, inasmuch as it renders the heart stout and bold, at the same time that it fuddles the head. It is said also, to be of great use to a Democratic candidate: because, a person having swallowed a glass of it, is ready to swallow anything else. {Edit. Bal.}

So much for not mixing drinks and politics.

In any case, "these two issues of the *Balance & Columbian Repository* of Hudson, New York, are two of the three primary signposts of the cocktail's holy grail…its origin," cocktail historian, author and collector Ted Haigh wrote in a 2009 article for *Imbibe* magazine. The third signpost Haigh cites is an 1803 use of the word in a newspaper called the *Farmer's Cabinet*, published in New Hampshire. That reference, although earlier than the one in the *Balance*, did not define it.

In his 2009 book, *Vintage Spirits and Forgotten Cocktails*, Haigh writes that in the *Farmer's Cabinet* the cocktail "was cited with barely contained contempt… as evidence of the intemperance of modern urban youth." The *Balance* reference, he notes, was "not particularly positive" either.

Cocktail historians, nevertheless, agree that the drink as defined in the *Balance* is significant, even if it came amid partisan political wrangling. "This [politics], not cocktails, provided the interest Americans followed with wonder," Haigh wrote in *Imbibe*. "Yet, it was in this setting that the cocktail was defined and introduced into the larger world."

In *Straight Up or On the Rocks*, Grimes introduces the Hudson *Balance* definition by noting that "[t]he mixing of whiskey, bitters, and sugar represents a turning point, as decisive for American drinking habits as the discovery of three-point perspective was for Renaissance painting. It is the beginning of the cocktail in modern form."

THE "HUDSON" COCKTAIL TODAY

What would a version of the drink that Harry Croswell defined in the *Balance* look and taste like today?

One obvious comparison is to the drink now called the Old Fashioned, though at certain times in recent history the link would have been unrecognizable.

In *Vintage Spirits and Forgotten Cocktails*, Haigh says the Old Fashioned stems from a drink called the Whiskey Cocktail, which in early renditions contained Croswell's ingredients: spirits (in this case, rye whiskey), plus water, sugar and bitters. It also contained an orange liqueur called curaçao. Later versions abandoned curaçao, substituting orange peel. "As the years wore on, it morphed into a veritable fruit cocktail with oranges, orange juice, cherries, and sometimes a piece of pineapple—oft times all mushed together or shaken together with blended whiskey."

Haigh, at the back of his book, rebuffs that muddle and offers a leaner version of the Old Fashioned that seems more in keeping with the Hudson original:

The Old Fashioned
Adapted from Vintage Spirits and Forgotten Cocktails *by Ted Haigh*

2 dashes bitters
½ teaspoon sugar
A few drops of water
2 ounces (or so) of rye or bourbon whiskey
A broad swathe of orange peel

Muddle the bitters, sugar and water in an Old Fashioned glass. Add a lump or two of ice, then the whiskey. Stir and serve with the orange peel. (The peel may be lightly muddled to express the oil.)

Another modern drinks author, Eric Felten, took a stab at an up-to-date version of the drink defined by Croswell in the *Balance* in his 2007 book, *How's Your Drink? Cocktail, Culture and the Art of Drinking Well*.

Felten's recipe follows a lively account of Croswell's antagonism to President Jefferson and a description of a case in which Jefferson sued Croswell for libel. (Jefferson ultimately lost.) Felten, drinks columnist for the *Wall Street Journal*, uses gin as the base for his Hudson *Balance*-inspired cocktail.

Bittered Gin Sling
From How's Your Drink? *by Eric Felten*

1 ½ ounces gin
¾ ounce sweet vermouth or sherry
½ ounce lemon juice
½ ounce simple (sugar) syrup
A dash or two of Angostura bitters
Soda water
Lemon peel

Shake all but the soda water with ice. Strain into a tumbler or highball glass over ice and top with soda. Garnish with lemon peel.

Reinventing Hudson's "Original" Cocktail

Of course, to find a modern interpretation of the original Hudson cocktail, it makes sense to visit Hudson itself.

Today, Hudson is still a vibrant river community, the kind of place where busy and relatively affluent folks from New York City and other metropolitan areas like to build weekend or summer getaways. That means it's filled with first-class bars and restaurants, aimed at a twenty-first-century audience that has grown up with the farm-to-table (locally sourced) food movement and the cocktail resurgence.

Jori Jayne Emde and her husband, James Beard award-winning chef Zack Pelaccio, are among the food and beverage stars to arrive in the Hudson area recently. They operate Fish & Game, a rustic yet classy place featuring set, full-course seasonal dinner and brunch menus. The search for a modern interpreter of the Hudson cocktail leads to Emde, who manages the bar program at Fish & Game.

Jori Jayne Emde, of Fish & Game restaurant in Hudson, created these cocktails inspired by the first definition of the cocktail in a Hudson newspaper. *Author's photo.*

She and Pelaccio met when she went to work as a sous chef at his Fatty 'Cue restaurant in New York City. They came Upstate after Pelaccio bought property in the rural community of Old Chatham in 2005. "There is no town in Old Chatham, so when we wanted to go out, we came to Hudson," Emde said. "We could easily see the potential with the historic buildings and just the vibe that was going on. We dug it." They opened Fish & Game in 2014 and later became partners in another spot, Back Bar, just a block or so away.

Emde, who grew up in Austin, Texas, is fascinated by Hudson's history, including its status as a wealthy whaling town in colonial days. (American whalers, it seems, brought their catch upriver to processors in Hudson to avoid contact with British authorities and their taxes.) Even as the town later fell on hard times, Emde says, the history is interesting. "I liked the seediness of it, all the brothels and bars and the dirty politicians as the wealth declined."

She has heard the story of the Hudson *Balance* and its place in cocktail history. Like others, she is not completely convinced that the cocktail was invented here. "It was certainly the first place where it was documented, and that's cool," she says. For this book, Emde prepared two cocktails that meet the definition of editor Harry Croswell's original cocktail.

The first is a version of a mint julep. Emde said she chose it partly because the julep was already a popular drink in 1806. Also, she notes that "the original juleps had bitters in them." Emde makes her own bitters at the farm in Old Chatham, under the name Lady Jayne's Alchemy. Here's her version of a julep, in the "original Hudson cocktail" style.

Hudson Mint Julep

From Jori Jayne Emde of Fish & Game, Hudson

5 to 6 mint leaves, torn
2 ounces bourbon
¼ ounce mint syrup
1 bar spoon of ginger bitters (Lady Jayne's Alchemy)

In a julep cup, muddle the mint leaves lightly to express the oils. Add the bourbon, mint syrup and ginger bitters. Fill half the julep cup with ice and then stir with a spoon until the cup develops a frost on the outside. Top off with more ice. Take a sprig of mint and slap it between the palms of your hands to express the oils and place in the drink for a beautiful garnish and refreshing nosegay while you sip.

The "Hudson" Mint Julep, created by Jori Jayne Emde of Fish & Game in Hudson. Its ingredients include bitters made by Emde's company, Lady Jayne's Alchemy. *Author's photo*.

Emde's second drink has a rum base. Rum was by far the most popular spirit in early American history. It was widely manufactured in New England—and even just north of Hudson in Albany—from Caribbean sugar and molasses. (We'll have more to say on rum in Upstate New York in the next chapter.)

Bittered Sling with Rum
From Jori Jayne Emde of Fish & Game, Hudson

1 ½ ounces white rhum agricole
1 ounce dark rum
½ ounce fennel bitters (Lady Jayne's Alchemy)
A few dashes of orange bitters
¼ ounce oleo saccharum (see note below)

Add all ingredients to an ice-filled shaker. Shake and strain into an ice-filled highball glass. Garnish with a piece of lime or orange peel and a brandy-soaked cherry.

Note: Oleo saccharum is made by mixing sugar and citrus peels, muddling them to express the oils and then letting it sit for about two weeks in a closed container at room temperature. "The sugar will draw out the lime oils from the peels, resulting in a very beautiful, almost citrus/floral note and the sugar will dissolve into a syrup," according to Emde.

THE LEWISTON LEGEND

Like Hudson, Lewiston, New York, sits on a great river—in this case the Niagara. The town is a little north of (and below) Niagara Falls. Lewiston is 340 miles from Hudson, but still in the vast area called Upstate New York.

And like Hudson, Lewiston has a claim to the origin of the cocktail. It centers on a woman named Catherine "Kitty" Hustler. Did this early tavern keeper pluck the feather off a passing rooster and use it to stir a drink? Was that the first "cock's tail" or "cocktail?"

They seem to believe the story in Lewiston. They repeat it often—on a downtown historical marker, in the words of an actress who plays Hustler in history-themed walking tours and in this bit of narrative produced by the Niagara County Historical Society:

Gravestone of Catherine "Kitty" Hustler in Lewiston, with pewter cocktail goblet and feather. *Author's photo.*

An interesting first in the annals of Niagara County is described in a story from the War of 1812. At that time, Thomas and Catherine Hustler operated a tavern in Lewiston that acquired a favorable international reputation among British, French and Americans, alike. Upon occasions, the Hustlers were even known to entertain a young naval officer named James Fenimore Cooper. Mr. and Mrs. Hustler stepped into bartending history when they supposedly began to serve drinks mixed from several liquors and stirred with a rooster's tail feather. Upon tasting the concoction, a young French officer was said to have stood and toasted Mrs. Hustler saying, "Viva la cocktail!" Historians have conjectured that it was the cocktail that spared the Hustler tavern when the British burned Lewiston during the War of 1812. Some say that British officers couldn't bear the thought of destroying the tavern where they first experienced this interesting libation. It is also assumed that James Fenimore Cooper, in his work, The Spy, *patterned two of his characters, Sergeant Hollister and Betty Flanagan, after Mr. and Mrs. Hustler, Niagara County's inventors of the cocktail.*

Note the word "supposedly" in this story. How much of it is true? There is evidence that the Hustlers ran a tavern in Lewiston. They seem to have arrived in the early 1800s—he was a Revolutionary War veteran and she served as a sutler, someone who delivered supplies, including liquor, to the troops.

The Lewiston Historical Society and Museum has several records related to them. One item, museum curator Pam Hauth points out, is a claim filed against the government by Thomas Hustler, who wanted to be compensated for having his property burned by the British. So perhaps that part of the story—that the British left the tavern standing—is in question. (There is no evidence he was paid.)

For the most part, the tale of the rooster's tail seems like just a good story. In the various versions told in and around Lewiston, details emerge or disappear and sometimes change. A version put out by the Lewiston Historical Society, for example, adds the suggestion that the drink itself was a "gin mixture." It also repeats the bit about the British not burning the tavern:

> *Hustler's Tavern in Lewiston was reportedly the only building left unscathed when the British invaded. Some say it was because the British officers remembered too many good times they had there sipping a "cocktail"—the drink that owner Catherine Hustler is credited with inventing when she stirred a "gin mixture" with the tail feather of a stuffed cockerel (a young male of the domestic fowl). She said it "warms both soul and body and is fit to be put in a vessel of diamonds."*

As ever, the tale keeps growing with each retelling. The historical society also packaged bits of the story of the Hustlers, the cocktail and Cooper and put them on a historic marker that stands today at the corner of Center and Eighth Streets, at the site where Hustler's Tavern once stood. This version adds some background to the creation of the first cocktail: "The story goes that British soldiers had raided a British commissary and brought Catherine some fowl which she roasted. For the feast, she decorated all the bottles and jars in the tavern with tail feathers. One guest called for a glass of the cocktail, and hence, the name was born."

If you visit Lewiston today, you don't have to read the cocktail story on a marker or in an archive. Thanks to the Lewiston Council on the Arts, the story of Kitty Hustler and her role in drinks history comes alive.

In recent years, local actress Kathryn Serianni began playing Kitty Hustler in a series of walking, or living history tours, produced by the arts council in conjunction with the historical society. History buffs and other

Marker from the Lewiston Historical Society at Center and Eight Streets in Lewiston, noting the site of Hustler's Tavern and the "birthplace of the cocktail." *Author's photo.*

visitors hear the tale (or tales) of the cocktail, usually from the starting point at Hustler's grave in the Village Cemetery, next to the First Presbyterian Church on Cayuga Street.

Serianni works from a couple of scripts. In one, she (as Kitty Hustler) takes the feather from a rooster to dress up a drink intended for the Marquis de Lafayette, a French military officer who had assisted the Americans in the Revolutionary War. (Lafayette did indeed visit Lewiston after the war. That much, the records support.) Lafayette enjoyed the new creation so much, Serianni/Hustler says, he jumped up and shouted, "Vive le Cocktail!"

Another of Serianni's scripts involves no celebrities. It's a more straightforward history of Hustler's Tavern and its role in the cocktail. During a performance at the site of Kitty Hustler's grave in June 2016, the account went like this:

> *I'm proud to say that we weren't a fancy place. But we didn't have to be. Most of our customers were soldiers from the fort or sailors waiting for their ships to be loaded and unloaded from Lewiston Landing. Now, Hustler's Tavern helped many of those first settlers spend those long winter evenings*

Lewiston actress Kathryn Serianni, portraying "Kitty" Hustler, said to be the inventor of the cocktail. *Lewiston Council on the Arts.*

here in the village of Lewiston. And one night—one special night—the customers were sitting around bored and starting to snipe at each other. So I thought I'd fix them up something special. I took one of my fine goblets and I put in a little gin and a little bit of mint and "something else" and I plucked the tail feather of a rooster that was lying dead on the bar. No matter how many times I told those hunters to leave their game outside, they'd bring them right in! Anyway, I plucked the tail off that rooster and gave the drink a stir and, lo and behold, the cocktail was invented. Right here in little Lewiston!

KITTY HUSTLER'S COCKTAIL: WHAT WAS IT?

We'll probably never know Hustler's original recipe (if there even was one). But we do know what a "gin mixture," as mentioned in Lewiston's historic annals and markers, could have been. In the early 1800s, in most taverns, inns and even some homes, you could find such drinks as gin toddies, gin sangarees and gin slings.

We've already provided author Eric Felten's version of a Bittered Gin Sling. Here, from the first-ever printed cocktail guide, compiled in 1862 by Upstate native and nineteenth-century celebrity bartender Jerry Thomas, are three gin mixtures already popular by that era.

A History

Gin Toddy
Adapted from How to Mix Drinks, *by Jerry Thomas (1862 edition)*

1 teaspoon sugar
½ wineglass water (1 to 2 ounces)
1 do. gin (2 ounces)
1 small lump ice

Mix in a small bar glass and stir with a spoon.

For a Gin Sling: Thomas's recipe is the same as for the Gin Toddy, but with sprinkled nutmeg on top.
For a Gin Sangaree: Follow the recipe for the Gin Toddy. Fill the glass two-thirds with ice and then float about a teaspoon of port wine on top.

You can search every bar and restaurant in Lewiston today and you won't find anyone who is using the feather of a rooster (dead or alive) to stir a mixed drink. That doesn't mean local bartenders aren't aware of the local lore.

"I have gone to every restaurant in Lewiston—everybody seems to know that the cocktail was invented here," said Eva Nicklas, a staffer for the Lewiston Council for the Arts who helps coordinate the tours that Serriani (as Kitty Hustler) and others lead around town.

The story even spawned a short-lived Lewiston Cocktail Festival to celebrate the historic events. (The festival was held through 2015, and organizers hope it will return.) Interestingly, the festival's website says Hustler "plucked a peacock quill from the back wall of a Lewiston bar she was tending," but as we've said, everyone in town seems to add their own element to the story.

The Water Street Landing restaurant overlooking the Niagara River helped spearhead the cocktail festival. "We started the cocktail fest to bring some swagger to the place where the cocktail was invented," said Matthew Ott, general manager. "We decided to let the bars compete to see who is the best in the home of the cocktail."

Water Street Landing won the contest in its first year with a drink called the Hibiscus Kiss, made with Absolut Hibiscus, a flavored vodka. Since that liquor is hard to find, Ott made us another drink to showcase the bar's (and Lewiston's) modern cocktail capabilities.

Pineapple Upside Down Cake
From Matthew Ott, Water Street Landing, Lewiston

1 ounce vodka
1 ounce coconut rum (Blue Chair Bay)
2 ounces pineapple juice
Maraschino cherry juice

Put the vodka and rum into an ice-filled shaker. Add the pineapple juice after first shaking it to foam it up. Shake and strain into a chilled martini glass. Using a straw, draw about an inch or two of maraschino cherry juice and then release it into the glass.

Note: Despite its tropical-sounding name, Blue Chair Bay rum has an Upstate connection. It is produced in Barbados but bottled at LiDestri Food & Beverage in Rochester. The brand is owned by country music superstar Kenny Chesney.

THE COCKTAIL, *THE SPY* AND JAMES FENIMORE COOPER

Catherine "Kitty" Hustler was real enough. But she's better known as the inspiration for a character in an early American work of fiction. She became "Betty Flanagan" in the novel *The Spy*, by James Fenimore Cooper. *The Spy* is a Revolutionary War story. The central plot is about a man suspected of, well, of being a British spy. In the book, Cooper describes Flanagan as "female sutler," "washerwoman" and "petticoat doctor" to the American troops in the vicinity of the "Four Corners," now Elmsford, Westchester County. (A sutler is someone who delivers supplies to army troops.)

Here's Cooper's description of this secondary, but memorable, character:

> *Betty was well known to every trooper in the corps, could call each by his Christian or nickname, as best suited her fancy; and, although absolutely intolerable to all whom habit had not made familiar with her virtues, was a genial favorite with these partisan warriors. Her faults were, a trifling love of liquor, excessive filthiness and a total disregard of all the decencies*

of language; her virtues, an unbounded love for her adopted country, perfect honesty when dealing on certain known principles with the soldiery, and great good nature.

Then Cooper comes to the point that lands Flanagan in the thick of the cocktail conversation:

Added to these, Betty had the merit of being the inventor of that beverage which is so well known, at the present hour, to all the patriots who make a winter's march between the commercial and political capitals of this great state, and which is distinguished by the name of "cocktail." Elizabeth Flanagan was peculiarly well qualified, by education and circumstances, to perfect this improvement in liquors, having been literally brought up on its principal ingredient, and having acquired from her Virginian customers the use of mint, from its flavor in a julep to the its height of renown in the article in question.

And according to Cooper, what did Betty Flanagan have to say about her own creation? "There's that within that's fit to be put in vissils of di'monds," she says, putting some dialect in the words often repeated today in Lewiston.

So, what's the connection between Elizabeth "Betty" Flanagan, Catherine "Kitty" Hustler and James Fenimore Cooper? And how do we get from Four Corners in Westchester County to Lewiston, on the Canadian border?

On the historic marker at the site of Hustler's Tavern, the corner of Center and Eighth Streets in Lewiston, the text describes Cooper's efforts to achieve literary success after the failure of his first novel, which was considered "unpatriotic":

Cooper, who had been a midshipman in the U.S. Navy, was stung by the criticism and he was determined his next book would breathe the very spirit of patriotism. He came to Lewiston for an extended stay in 1821 to write The Spy *and was a frequent visitor at Hustler's Tavern. He befriended the owners, Thomas and Catherine Hustler, and was so amused by their personalities he included the couple as the characters Sergeant Hollister and Elizabeth "Betty" Flanagan, in his new novel.*

This book, the marker states, was a success. As history, it leaves some question marks. This account, like many others, puts the year of Cooper's stay in Lewiston as 1821. Many other accounts say he stayed there—and encountered Kitty Hustler—during the War of 1812. That would mean his visit could have been no later than early 1815 or earlier.

Of course, history and fiction often intertwine. Consider a fanciful historical narrative titled "Something of Yesterday," one of the source materials used by Serriani for her portrayal of Hustler.

It starts with a description of the anger and disappointment that the people of Lewiston felt in 1821, when their town lost out to the nearby community of Lockport in the selection of a county seat for Niagara. On this particular night, the men in the tavern weren't drinking much. The account gives another version of Hustler's "cock-tail" drink. "Into the tankard she pours a large allowance of gin and some drops of herbed wine and to mix the two she plucks the tail feather of a stuffed cock pheasant....Her blue eyes now dancing she slides the tankard across the oaken table...'Drink yee,' says she, ''twill warm both sowl and body.'"

And where was James Fenimore Cooper? "Aside and alert in a corner sits a traveler most interested in the evening's proceedings," this story continues. "Before the sun comes up, Fennimore [*sic*] Cooper, writing at a small desk in an upstairs room, fashions Betty Flanagan of his novel, "The Spy," from this very Katherine Hustler of Lewiston, who gave to the land its first cock-tail."

New York Times writer William Grimes, before writing his 2001 cocktail history, *Straight Up or On the Rocks*, offered this assessment of the Betty (or Betsy) Flanagan legend in a *New York Times* column dated August 25, 1991:

> *The word cocktail has inspired perhaps the most notorious fraud of all—the Flanagan Fallacy. Virtually every account of the cocktail's origins drags in Betsy Flanagan, an innkeeper during the Revolutionary War who stirred a drink with a rooster tail and dubbed it a cocktail. Some versions place the inn at Four Corners, in Westchester County, N.Y.; others locate the sacred ground a few miles away in Elmsford. For the real location, turn to Chapter 16 of James Fenimore Cooper's "Spy," published in 1821 but set in the 1780's. There, Flanagan and feather first appear, as real as fiction.*

One more thing about Kitty Hustler, the linchpin for this bit of Upstate cocktail lore, both fact and fiction. She appears to have been a "wild woman," according to Eva Nicklas of the Lewiston Council of the Arts. Hustler's roles as a supplier of goods to troops and the keeper of a tavern would have kept her from being considered genteel in those days, underscored by Cooper's references to the character Betty Flanagan's drinking, dirtiness and indecent language.

A History

Hustler's grave is well marked in the Lewiston village cemetery, next to her husband's. Along with her name and date of death, it bears this inscription:

Traveler as you are passing by
As you are now so once was I
As I am now so you must be
Prepare for death and follow me

To confirm Nicklas's point about her character, many around Lewiston add these lines:

To follow her I'm not content,
until I know which way she went

2

DISTILLING, RUM AND THE HUDSON VALLEY

Spirits: The Key Ingredient

You can't make a cocktail without at least one distilled spirit as an ingredient.

As we've seen, Upstate New York may have a fairly strong claim—or at least a few stories to tell—about the origins of the cocktail. But it certainly can't claim to be the birthplace of hard liquor or distilled spirits. What's more, New York doesn't have a strong connection to a specific, or signature, spirit. It's not the birthplace of bourbon—that's Kentucky, of course. It's not well known as an original source of American rye whiskey; Pennsylvania and Maryland lay claim to rye. New Jersey built a reputation for applejack (a liquor made by distilling hard apple cider). Tennessee is the home of sour mash.

And yet early European settlers in New York State certainly brought a love of distilled spirits with them. They came from the Netherlands, England, Ireland, Scotland and other nations that had strong spirits traditions.

The earliest European immigrants to New York were the Dutch—who would become well known for their gin, or jenever. But that's probably not what the first Dutch settlers were making, according to Gary "Gaz" Regan and Mardee Haidin Regan, whose research into American distilling has been published in *The Book of Bourbon and Other Fine American Whiskeys*, with portions republished on the website of the Distilled Spirits Council of the United States (DISCUS).

"In 1640, William Kieft, the Director General of the New Netherland Colony, decided that liquor should be distilled on Staten Island," the Regans wrote. "His master distiller, Wilhelm Hendriksen, is said to have used corn and rye to make liquor, and since the Dutch didn't develop a formula for gin until 10 or so years later, he must have been making some form of whiskey."

DISTILLED SPIRITS: WHAT ARE THEY?

Alcoholic beverages come in many varieties: beer, wine, hard cider, vodka, brandy, gin, rum, whiskey, cordials and more. Some are fermented. Some are distilled.

Distilled spirits (aka hard liquors) are the main subjects of this book (along with the cocktails made from them), although fermented alcohol beverages are also used in mixed drinks. They are related. In fact, you must ferment before you can distill. Here's a simple explanation:

All alcoholic beverages start with sugar. Add yeast to sugars diluted in a liquid solution, and you get fermentation. That's the basic way to make beer, wine or hard cider. The fermentation creates alcohol and provides essential elements to the final aroma and flavor. For wine and hard cider, the natural sugars in fruits like grapes or apples can be the base for fermentation. Beer takes another initial step. Grains like barley must be malted (allowed to germinate) to release the sugars. Then fermentation can take place.

Distilled spirits require a follow-up step: the fermented alcohol is heated to its boiling point, turns to steam, and then portions are recondensed as a stronger, purer liquid product. Stills make spirits from already fermented beverages, like beer, wine or cider. The result is many times stronger (higher in alcohol). You lose a lot of volume in distilling (and even more in the aging process). That's one reason distilled spirits are more expensive.

Some distilled spirits are clear—like vodka and gin and even white whiskey and white rum. These are not aged in wood. Aging in wooden barrels yields what are often known as "brown spirits," like most whiskey, amber or dark rum, brandy and more.

The different categories of spirits are typically based on the base ingredient they're made from. Rum, for example, is made from either molasses or sugar cane syrup (with cane sugar the base for both). Whiskey is made from grain: corn, wheat, rye, barley or a combination. Vodka can be made from just about anything: corn, wheat, potatoes, apples, grapes, honey or more. Gin can be made from any of the same base ingredients as vodka but with additional herbs or "botanicals" for aroma and flavor.

NATIVE AMERICANS, COLONISTS AND REBELS

The European settlers found much of the raw produce they could make into beer, wine and liquor already under cultivation by the Native Americans living in what is now Upstate New York. But it appears the native peoples of the region—the Iroquois (Haudenosaunee), Algonquin, Huron and others—did not routinely make alcoholic spirits from them.

The alcoholic beverages produced by North America's indigenous people—pulque or mezcal, for example—seem to have been found mostly in what is now Mexico and the American Southwest. Not so in the Northeast, writes Patrick J. Abbott, in a paper published through the University of Colorado Denver.

"Alcoholic beverage use in this region (the Northeast) is sparsely documented," Abbott noted, citing multiple sources on Native American culture and history. "There is some evidence that the Huron made a mild beer made from corn.…They, apparently, placed unripe corn into a stagnant pool of water, left if for several months and from this made a fermented gruel. This was drunk at tribal feasts. Reference has been made to 'maple wine' and 'sassafras beer' but it appears that these beverages were used before fermentation."

"The French, Dutch, and English colonists quickly settled this land," Abbott continued, "lured by the land's abundant resources. In the trade that ensued, alcohol emerged as a vital and often destructive commodity. The colonists that immigrated from Europe placed a great deal of importance on their alcoholic beverages." Those beverages could be fermented or distilled. Beer was popular among the Europeans and, in the Northeast, so was hard cider, fermented like beer and made from apple juice.

In their discussion on early distilling, the Regans note that early settlers made beer and imported wine, brandy, sherry and other products that could withstand the long trip from Europe. "But still, these early Americans weren't content," the Regans wrote. "They wanted their own

SPIRITS & COCKTAILS OF UPSTATE NEW YORK

liquor.…Like the first beers and wines, the first liquors made here used a variety of ingredients—berries, plums, potatoes, apples, carrots, and grain—anything that had the power to attract yeast and then ferment. The spirits they made were probably not the smoothest of potions, mind you—but they were liquor all the same."

Early American settlers probably drank much of their liquor straight—a dram of whiskey, a shot of rum, a pony or jigger of gin. But there certainly were mixed drinks. One of the simplest was a mix of hard cider, made throughout the Northeast, and rum, manufactured in large quantities in nearby New England—and, as we shall see, in Albany and other parts of New York. The drink was called the Stone Fence, or Stone Wall—maybe because rum, hard cider and rocks were all common in what is now Upstate New York.

In an essay for *Esquire* magazine, cocktail historian David Wondrich tells the story of this drink and connects it to the battle for Upstate New York's Fort Ticonderoga during the American Revolution.

Before the revolution, Wondrich notes, there had been occasional skirmishes between the men of Vermont—the famous Green Mountain Boys led by Ethan Allen—and those of the neighboring state to the west, the "Yorkers."

The Vermonters, based in Bennington, had been having "a grand old time fighting the Yorkers," Wondrich writes. With the outbreak of war against the British, "they were after bigger game. They were going to take Ticonderoga." "What do you drink before taking on a garrison of well-entrenched professional soldiers, a garrison that has 100 cannon to your none, with nothing more than a gang of high-spirited part-timers?" Wondrich continues. "According to the Green Mountain Boys, you drink cider. Hard cider. In fact, hard cider with a hefty shot of rum in it. A lot of it."

That, in essence, is the Stone Fence, or Stone Wall.

Stone Fence
From "How to Make a Stone Fence" by David Wondrich, Esquire *magazine*

2 ounces dark rum
Hard cider

Pour the rum into a pint glass, add 1 or 2 ice cubes and fill with hard cider.

Note: "This drink, otherwise known as a Stone Wall, can also be made with, in order of authenticity, applejack, rye whiskey, or anything else in place of the rum," Wondrich says.

ALBANY AND THE AGE OF RUM

Rum? Isn't rum a tropical spirit? Where would early New Yorkers get rum?

In colonial times and through the Revolutionary War, it turns out, rum was America's most popular spirit. It was, originally, shipped in from the West Indies, as far back as the 1670s and '80s, when it was an inexpensive import. "Almost overnight, rum found its way into every aspect of colonial life," writes author Wayne Curtis in his 2006 book, *And a Bottle of Rum: A History of the New World in Ten Cocktails.*

"A colonist would toss back a dram in the morning to shake off the night chills and to launch the day in proper form," Curtis explains. "Rum was embraced in sickness and in health, and for better or worse." It was, Curtis notes, used to cure ills and sometimes "doled out liberally to citizens who helped raise a barn or meeting house."

Before 1700, according to Curtis, most rum in the colonies was imported. After that, it was more likely that a colonist's tipple was distilled domestically. Rum distilling was most prevalent in Massachusetts and other parts of New England, but Curtis notes that the New York colony was home to seventeen rum distillers by 1750.

If you remember your high school history, you'll recall that rum was one of the key elements of what teachers called the Triangle Trade. Rum distilled in the American colonies was shipped to West Africa, where it could be used to barter for slaves, who were taken to the West Indies, where they worked in the sugarcane fields. The molasses made from the sugar was then shipped to New England and the middle Atlantic colonies like New York, where distillers turned it into rum.

Curtis, citing other historians, writes that rum's role in the Triangle Trade was probably exaggerated and suggests that New England merchants had little involvement with the notorious slave trade. Yet rum distilled from island molasses did become a big business in the Northeast, including Upstate New York, right through the earliest days of the American republic.

At the dawn of the twenty-first century, a modern project—the building of a parking garage in downtown Albany—uncovered an archaeological find that opened a window into the history of rum distilling in Upstate New York.

The site is the place now known as Quackenbush Square, in the heart of Albany near the Hudson River. In the 1600s, that location was just outside the Dutch colonial settlement of Beverwyck. Digging on the site of the planned parking garage uncovered two things: evidence of brick-making operation during the Dutch period (the mid-1600s), and well-preserved remains of what turned out to be two rum distilleries that operated from the 1750s to the early 1800s, covering the time of British, and then American, governance.

The archaeological excavation took place in the winter of 2000. Among the items recovered were nine large fermentation vessels, or vats, two of which are now housed in the New York State Museum. As part of its excavation, the firm Hartgen Archeological Associates of Rensselaer, New York, prepared an extensive report, published in October 2005. It detailed the physical findings at the site, accompanied by observations on the history of rum distilling in early America and in the Albany region.

"The amount of material in that site that was left intact was really unusual," Justin DiVirgilio, Hartgen's president and one the report's authors, said in a 2017 interview. "It would be unusual in that area to find house sites that intact, and so a distillery is that much more unusual."

The Hartgen report is comprehensive in its archaeological analysis and its historic context. Its major conclusion was that although the Albany region of the New York colony still had a predominantly Dutch culture when the distilleries were built, the construction and operation of the distilleries shows it was giving way to British, and ultimately American, influence.

The first of the two distilleries on the site was built about 1759, about eighty years after the British seized control of the New York colony. Though the distillery founders were Dutch, the distilling complex (which the report calls the Douw-Quackenbush Still House after the early owners) was built in an English style, the archaeologists found. And it made rum, much more popular with the British than the Dutch colonials.

"That members of long-settled, Dutch Albany families set out to produce a quintessentially British drink is evidence of the changing times," according to the Hartgen report. The report continues:

> When it came to alcohol, the Dutch preferred beer, wine, and brandy. The reason for the popularity of rum in Albany reflected a change in the makeup of the citizenry relating to the colonial wars, the Revolutionary

Drawing of the historic Quackenbush stillhouse site in Albany. *Rendering by Walter L. Wheeler, Hartgen Archeological Associates, Rensselaer, New York.*

War, and the arrival of an increasing number of New England Yankees during the post-colonial period. Yankees had enjoyed New England rum for nearly a century years before the Quackenbush-Douw distillery steamed off its first batch. British army regulars and New England volunteers alike expected their daily ration of rum while they garrisoned the city or used it as a jumping off point for attacks against French targets. Furthermore, there was a colonial act forbidding the distilling of locally grown grain into liquor. So, if there were to be a distillery in Albany, it was almost a certainty that its product would be rum.

The report, using evidence from the archaeological site, offers a glimpse into how rum was made at the Quackenbush site:

Rum production was dependent on a steady supply of water and molasses. The still-house was ideally situated for the convenient delivery of both. It was located near the Hudson River along a lane (Quackenbush Street) extending from the riverbank to Watervliet Street….Molasses was mixed with the water to provide the sugar necessary for fermentation to occur. It was imported from the West Indies to Albany in large casks, most commonly in hogsheads (100 to 110 gallons)….It is estimated that when the distillery operated at full capacity that it consumed up to 50 hogsheads of molasses per month.

The finished product was then packaged in either casks or bottles, depending on whether it was intended to be sold wholesale or retail, Hartgen reports, citing contemporary reports in the *Albany Gazette* newspaper. "Typical wholesale cask sizes for 'Common Rum' were the 'Hogshead or Barrel,'" the *Gazette* reported in 1790. Rum intended for retail sale was typically placed in glass "wine" bottles, the Hartgen report says, noting that "the remains of numerous glass wine bottles were disposed in the fermentation vats after the Douw-Quackenbush still-house was abandoned."

In the mid-point of its existence, in the 1780s, then-owner Daniel Hale noted that the Douw-Quackenbush still house could "clearly make 220 gallons per day." But it's unlikely that distilling was a year-round enterprise in Albany, due to the occasional shortage of molasses and the freezing of the Hudson River.

The number of rum distilleries in New York never rivaled the number in nearby New England, but it did grow in the 1700s. The Hartgen report shows there were two distilleries in the colony of New York in 1737, growing to three by 1747, six by 1749 and seventeen by 1768.

In time, the rum distilleries at Quackenbush, and almost everywhere else in the Northeast, began to close up, ending their run in the first decades of the nineteenth century. "If the arrival of Yankees in Albany in the late 18th century explained the rise of rum, it was the arrival of other immigrant groups with other preferences when it came to alcohol that contributed to its demise," according to the Hartgen report. "Among them the Irish, Germans, and English tended to prefer beer when it came to libation, and the number of breweries in the city proliferated to meet the burgeoning demand. Eventually, there was not enough demand for locally made rum to maintain even one distillery."

There was another factor in the decline of rum distilling: the migration of settlers to the west, driven in part by the construction of the Erie Canal across Upstate New York. "Following the Revolution," the report says, "the westward movement across the Appalachians encouraged the manufacture of a drink that could be made from locally produced grain." It was a matter of simple economics. "The expansion of agriculture and the construction of canals to carry produce to market drastically lowered prices [for grain-based spirits]."

That migration, along with American taste preferences, spelled the end of rum made in New York State—at least until the early twenty-first century.

Albany Rum: A Twenty-First Century Return

It's no accident that John Curtin decided to make rum at the distillery he co-founded in 2011 at Quackenbush Square in downtown Albany. He had followed the news of the archaeological discovery and knew the site had been home to two historic rum distilleries. He read up on the history of rum distilling in colonial America, so he was sure Albany Distilling Company would take a cue from that history and make rum.

In its report on the excavation of the historic Quackenbush Still House in downtown Albany, Hartgen Archeological Associates dug up this recipe for an American-made rum, dated 1729:

> *Fill a large Vat or Vessel near three Parts full of River-water, to which add as much new Molasses, or till it be so strong as it will bear up an Egg, (which will require about one third part of the latter) then beat them up very well, till a froth begin to appear on the surface, and let the Liquor stand fermenting for the space of twelve or fourteen days, more or less, till it cease working; then skim it clean and put it into your Still.*

To be clear, Albany Distilling does not follow this recipe, exactly. It certainly does not use unfiltered Hudson River water channeled directly into a vat. But the bit about the egg? That's a little closer. "We looked at that old recipe, and coincidentally, the density of a yeast fermented molasses and water solution for the style of rum we wanted is about the same as a raw

Quackenbush Still House Original Albany Rum. *Albany Distilling Company.*

egg," Curtin said. "So that's where we got the ratio for our wash." (The wash refers to the liquid after fermentation but before distillation.)

Albany Distilling, co-owned by Curtin and Rick Sicari, today makes two rums under the Quackenbush Still House label: Albany Rum, an unaged, clear white spirit; and Albany Amber, aged in oak for a deeper color and a taste with hints of spice and vanilla.

"The (original) Quackenbush Still House produced an unaged rum from Caribbean molasses and Hudson River water, fermented with wild yeasts in huge, open wooden vessels," Albany Distilling notes on its website. "We use modern equipment, better yeast, and a more suitable water supply, but we follow the same recipe and use the methods of our predecessors."

In the 1750s, Curtin points out, the Quackenbush still would have been hand-hammered copper, with an open fire underneath. Modern distilling is much more controlled. Many modern spirits makers distill two or three times to make their products smoother and higher in proof (alcohol). Albany Distilling distills its rum just once, as distillers would have in the eighteenth century, but it manages to yield 81 to 84 proof, Curtin said. It's bottled at 80 proof (40 percent alcohol).

"It's not quite as earthy as the original, but it is earthy, with a lot more flavor than standard rums today," he noted.

Albany Distilling makes other products, including a line of aged whiskeys under the Ironweed label. They include Bourbon, Rye and Straight Malt Whiskey (with barley, wheat and oats). They are named for the Pulitzer Prize–winning novel *Ironweed*, written by Albany native William Kennedy and largely set in the Albany area during the Great Depression. The company also has two clear (or unaged) whiskeys.

In 2016, Albany Distilling teamed up with a local roaster, Death Wish Coffee Co. of Round Lake, to introduce Death Wish Coffee Flavored Vodka.

Here's a recipe using Albany Distilling's Quackenbush Still House Albany Amber, concocted by noted Albany bartender Robert Mack.

The Doctor Cocktail
From Robert Mack

1 ½ ounces Quackenbush Amber Rum (or more, to taste)
¾ ounce Kronan Swedish Punsch (cachaça is a good substitute)
¾ ounce fresh lime juice (Key lime if possible)

Combine all ingredients in shaker with ice. Shake and strain into large coupe. Garnish with Key lime wheel.

WHEN PUNCH WAS IN ITS HEYDAY

Before leaving Albany and its rum history, let's take a turn around the punch bowl.

In the eighteenth century, when Albany-made rum was at its height, so was the fashion for alcoholic drinks called punch. They were often—though not always—served in decorative punch bowls. The Albany Institute of History and Art has many from old Capital Region families in its collection and, in February 2014, hosted a special exhibit of them called "Potent Potables."

"By the eighteenth century it [punch] had become the drink of choice in England and the American colonies where punch making was considered a social accomplishment," the narrative accompanying the exhibition read. "Albany newspapers from the late eighteenth century, when punch was at its heyday, ran front page advertisements from local merchants offering consumers a host of choices for their favorite punch recipe," the exhibit notes add. The institute collected some of those recipes, connected to some of the Albany area's oldest families. Each is accompanied by a note from the exhibition.

Lime Rum Shrub
From the Collection of the Albany Institute of History and Art

Fresh lime juice
Sugar
Water
Dark Rum
(2 parts rum to 1 ½ parts lime cordial)

Mix fresh lime juice with simple syrup made from sugar and water.

Note: "Rum, brandy, and limes were also popular import items for Albany as evidenced by the frequent appearance of these goods in mid-eighteenth century family account ledgers," the art institute's narrative states. "A punch like Lime Rum Shrub (from the Arabic shurb, meaning drink) made from sugar, water, dark rum, and fresh lime juice, not unlike the modern gimlet, was a favorite drink of the Van Rensselaers."

Punch bowl, circa 1801, bearing the initials of original owner, Kiliaen K. Van Rensselaer, an Albany lawyer and congressman. *From the collection of the Albany Institute of History and Art, Albany, New York.*

Regents Punch

From the Collection of the Albany Institute of History and Art

4 pounds raisins
2 quarts green tea
1 quart lemon juice
3 quarts champagne
2 quarts hock (German white wine)
1 quart curaçao
2 quarts Madeira
1 quart brandy
2 quarts seltzer
1 pint Jamaica rum
Fruit

Macerate raisins in tea and lemon juice and allow to stand overnight. Add other ingredients and serve cold.

Note: This recipe came from John Van Schaick Lansing Pruyn, who served as chancellor of the New York State Board of Regents. A bowl in the art institute's collection owned by Pruyn had once belonged to early New York governor Daniel Tompkins; in 1824, it was used during a ball in the state capitol to honor the Marquis de Lafayette.

The Pioneer Spirit Today: Hudson Valley Distillers

Before our history of Upstate New York distilled spirits and cocktails heads west, let's visit a modern alcoholic beverage maker just south of the town of Hudson, where our cocktail story started. Here, in Clermont, we find Hudson Valley Distillers, owned and operated by Tom Yozzo and Chris Moyer.

"We grow apples in the Hudson Valley and always have," said Yozzo, a retired police officer. "They used to grow rye here. Corn came along later. All can be made into distilled spirits and all have been at one time or another in this area."

Co-owner Tom Yozzo in the still house at Hudson Valley Distillers, Clermont. *Author's photo.*

Yozzo and Moyer keep alive the pioneering spirit, using local grain and fruit to make their products. As Yozzo attested, "We do our own thing." They started production in 2013, began selling their products in 2015 and opened the adjacent tasting room in 2015. Their lineup includes vodka, gin and whiskey. Their Imperial Whiskey is based on the same grains and malts (mash bill) used at the nearby Chatham Brewery for its Imperial Porter. (It's essentially a porter, minus the hops, that's distilled and aged into a whiskey.)

Hudson Valley also makes applejack, one of the oldest distilled spirits in Upstate New York. Traditional applejack was made by "freeze distilling" hard apple cider to make a concentrated beverage higher in alcohol. At Hudson Valley, Yozzo and Moyer use modern distilling methods and equipment to produce three versions: Adirondack Applejack, aged in white oak barrels; Hardscrabble Applejack, a smoky example made in heavily charred oak barrels; and Fine Shine Applejack, an unaged, clear variety. All are made with Hudson Valley apples.

Next to the distillery, Hudson Valley Distillers operates a tasting room, the Cocktail Grove. It makes drinks using its own spirits, of course, and also maintains that pioneer spirit by concocting its own mixers and other ingredients, using as much local produce as possible. It also has a light food menu.

Here are two recipes using Hudson Valley spirits and mixers.

Nonny Rose
From Hudson Valley Distillers

2 ounces Hudson Valley Adirondack Applejack
½ ounce grenadine
½ ounce lemon juice
Slice of lemon

Stir the ingredients with ice and strain into a cocktail glass.

Note from the tasting room menu: "A take on the gangster, Jack Rose, this cocktail is like Tom's great-grandmother. Not too sweet, but packs a punch!"

Hudson "Apple" Loosa
From Hudson Valley Distillers

1 ½ ounces Hudson Valley Spirits Grove Vodka
Splash of lime juice
Ginger beer
Slice of lime

Add vodka and lime juice to ice-filled cup or glass, top with ginger beer and garnish with lime.

Note: The vodka is made from Hudson Valley apples.

3

WHISKEY AND THE "WEST"

We were forty miles from Albany
Forget it I never shall
What a terrible storm we had that night
On the E-ri-e Canal
O-o-oh the E-Ri-e was a-rising
The gin was a-getting low;
And I scarcely think
We'll get a drink
Till we get to Buffalo-o-o
Till we get to Buffalo
—an old Erie Canal song

WHERE THE SPIRITS FLOWED: THE ERIE CANAL

Nothing in the nineteenth century did more to impact the growth of Upstate New York—and its burgeoning whiskey and spirits trade—than the Erie Canal. The canal itself linked Buffalo, on Lake Erie in the west, to Albany and the Hudson River in the east. When it opened in 1825, officials led by Governor DeWitt Clinton poured some Lake Erie water into the harbor at the mouth of the Hudson River, in New York City, in a ceremony marking the "wedding of the waters."

Canal travel was made possible by water, but history shows the Erie was also well lubricated by whiskey. During the 1820s, as the canal was being

Sign outside the Erie Canal Museum, Syracuse. *Author's photo.*

dug, "America was reeling through the most phenomenal drinking binge in its history," author Jack Kelly writes in *Heaven's Ditch: God, Gold and Murder on the Erie Canal*, a 2016 account that explores the canal and the social upheavals of its time, including those related to drink, temperance and religion.

As we've seen, immigration, westward migration and the canal helped bring an end to the rum distilleries of Albany and elsewhere in New York. But that didn't bring an end to distilling. Whiskey took over, partly because it was cheaper to make that spirit from the state's own wheat and corn crops than to make rum from imported molasses.

That wasn't the only economic benefit.

"Western farmers who grew barley, corn, and rye found it more profitable to ferment and distill their crops into strong liquor than to ship the grain to market," Kelly writes. "Whiskey was plentiful and cheap....By the middle of the decade [the 1820s], more than a thousand distillers were operating in New York state."

It began even as the canal was under construction. Many independent contractors were engaged to dig sections, and they had to hire labor. "It was up to the contractor to hire the men to do the work," according to *The Erie Canal*, a straightforward history written in 1964 by Ralph K. Andrist. "He was also expected to put up a shack big enough to sleep twenty-four to 40 men; to supply them with horses, capers, shovels and other equipment; to feed them and give them their daily ration of whiskey; and to pay them."

Among the jobs on some canal-digging crews was a position called the "jigger boss," Andrist notes. One canal contractor, a man named JJ McShane from Ireland's County Tipperary, "paid a fair wage—75 cents a day—and provided a 'jigger boss,' a man who went along the line dispensing whiskey to the workers several times a day."

Digging the canal was hard. "It was backbreaking work," Andrist writes. "Every bit of dirt had to be dug up with picks and shovels from nearby fields and hills, and hauled by wheelbarrows and horse-drawn carts to the valley." The contractors hiring workers had to make it sound a little more appealing. "'Would you care for a fine job upstate?' the hiring boss would ask Irish immigrants arriving in New York City. 'Working conditions are very good, with roast beef guaranteed twice a day, regular whiskey rations and wages 80 cents.'"

Once the canal was completed, whiskey and other spirits took their place among the many goods shipped between Buffalo and Albany. "Boats from the west carried the produce of farm and forest to the cities of the East Coast: potatoes, apples, cider, wheat and milled flour, whiskey, live turkeys, lumber and precious furs," Andrist writes.

And whiskey and distilled spirits were available along the route, Andrist's account attests: "A captain could tie up in front of [canal-side shops] and buy a firkin—a small cask—of salt mackerel or a bushel of oats, have a horse shod or get a gallon of whiskey, and pick up the latest news at the same time. There was a grocery store, and sometimes two, at every lock—and in those days, they sold much more than food. Almost all of them carried liquor which, being very cheap, was drunk in great quantities."

Passengers could drink their fill. In *Heaven's Ditch*, Kelly writes of the delays that travelers endured during the many tedious stops the boats had to make when passing through locks. "During the wait, many passengers hop off the boat to stretch their legs. They can be pretty sure of a chance to grab a glass of whiskey. Locks are favorite spots for locals to set up small grocery shops that sell drinks and sundries."

Temperance advocates were alarmed by the numbers, according to Kelly. "Reformers insisted in 1835 that there were some 1,500 drinking establishments along the canal, an astounding average of one every quarter mile. In Lockport [near Buffalo], two dozen bars crowded together within fifty feet of the locks."

Replica packet boat outside the Erie Canal Museum, Syracuse. *Author's photo.*

The Erie Canal Museum and Visitor's Center, Syracuse. *Author's photo.*

Over time, attitudes on all this drinking evolved. Early on, Andrist notes, "it was believed then [1825] that whiskey helped ward off the combination of fever and chills," which was just one of the reasons whiskey was supplied to canal diggers and boat crews.

But the temperance movement gained traction as the nineteenth century wore on. "Frequent drunkenness led to violence aboard the boats, which spilled over into the towns," Andrist writes. He continues:

> So flawed was the Erie Canal by immorality that many began to refer to it as the "Big Ditch of Iniquity." Believing the moral decline was a result of excessive drinking, New York canal commissioners tried in 1833 to prohibit liquor use by canal workers, but it was impossible to enforce. At least one company of canal boat owners announced that they would employ only "men who do not swear nor drink ardent spirits."

Eventually, the growing temperance movement spurred the drive that led to Prohibition in 1919. In the meantime, however, both the production and consumption of alcohol continued in Upstate New York and elsewhere.

COCKTAILS ALONG THE ERIE TODAY

The "old" Erie Canal—and much of the original route—had ceased operations by the early twentieth century. It was replaced by the larger, more efficient New York State Barge Canal, which combined some older sections with new wider, straighter and deeper ones. In some cases, old sections remain as sleepy backwaters or quiet parks, while others have been filled in.

One of the filled-in sections is the stretch now called Erie Boulevard, running through Syracuse and its suburbs. That's where Jeremy Hammill, a modern mixologist, creates and mixes cocktails at the Scotch 'n Sirloin, a restaurant and steakhouse on Erie Boulevard East, in the Syracuse suburb of DeWitt. He and a friend, Scott Murray, also run a small company manufacturing cocktail bitters, called Mad Fellows.

Among the drinks on Hammill's cocktail list at the Scotch 'n Sirloin is one he called the Erie Boulevardier, a spin on the classic Boulevardier. A Boulevardier is a combination of bourbon, red vermouth and Campari or other Italian bitter liqueur. (It's similar to a Negroni, which uses gin instead of bourbon.)

A Mule Named Sal, an Erie Canal–themed cocktail by bartender Jeremy Hammill, at the Erie Canal Museum in Syracuse. *Photo by Dennis Nett.*

We asked Hammill to create a couple of Erie Canal–themed drinks for this book. For our photos, he mixed them up at the replica nineteenth-century bar in the Erie Canal Museum, which sits along Erie Boulevard in downtown Syracuse. The museum features a replica packet boat and many period items and exhibits and is located in a former Erie Canal "weighlock," where boats would put in to have their cargos weighed.

Here are Hammill's Erie Canal cocktails. Each uses exclusively Upstate New York ingredients.

A Mule Named Sal
From Jeremy Hammill of the Scotch 'n Sirloin, DeWitt

1½ ounces 1911 Established Vodka
1 dropper of Mad Fellows Spiced Apple Bitters (or a splash of fresh-pressed cider)
Saranac Ginger Beer
A Cortland apple for garnish

Fill a Moscow Mule cup (a small copper cup with a handle) with ice. Pour in vodka and then add the bitters or cider. Top with ginger beer. Garnish with apple.

The Low Bridge, an Erie Canal–themed cocktail created by bartender Jeremy Hammill that uses all New York ingredients, at the Erie Canal Museum in Syracuse. *Photo by Dennis Nett.*

Low Bridge

From Jeremy Hammill of the Scotch 'n Sirloin, DeWitt

1 ounce Albany Distilling Death Wish coffee vodka
1 ounce Black Button 4 Grain Bourbon
1 ounce cinnamon/clove infused simple syrup (note)
1 dropper of Mad Fellows Mulled Spice bitters
½ ounce heavy cream
Freshly grated cinnamon

Chill a martini glass or coupe. Fill a shaker glass with ice and then add all ingredients except the cinnamon. Shake well and strain into martini glass or coupe. Sprinkle on cinnamon for garnish.

Note: To make the simple syrup, boil 2 cups water with 1 broken up cinnamon stick and 4 whole cloves to extract the flavor. When it smells right, add 2 cups sugar and boil to dissolve. Let cool and strain into a clean bottle. Will hold for a month in the refrigerator. (It can be reduced, but always use equal parts water and sugar.)

Temperance, Taxes and "Fiery Stuff"

Rum distilling, which had thrived in Albany and the Hudson Valley in eastern New York in the 1700s, faded by the early 1800s. But thanks in large part to the Erie Canal and other westward trails, distilling of other spirits continued across Upstate New York, moving west along with the onrush of new settlers who built communities out of the wilderness.

"It was recorded in 1810 that Onondaga County had two breweries," according to a 1997 pamphlet titled "Bottoms Up!" from the Onondaga Historical Association in Syracuse. "The average price for their product was $.17 per gallon and together they turned out about 7,200 gallons that year. It was a relatively minor enterprise, when compared to the 26 liquor distilleries in the county which produced nearly 80,000 gallons annually. Liquor sold at an average of $.80 per gallon!"

That scenario didn't last, as breweries eventually overtook distilleries through the nineteenth century. The influx of German, Irish and other immigrants had something to do with that, but so did the rise of the temperance movement, as liquor was considered more evil than beer. Still, the distilled spirits industry did thrive. The rise of distilling took place all across Upstate New York, from the Hudson Valley west to the Great Lakes and up toward Canada.

It would be difficult to provide a record of every settler who set up a still or every entrepreneur who started a distilling business in Upstate New York. To provide a glimpse of how the distilling industry did emerge in the region, we'll take a close look at one community: Skaneateles, a small village in Onondaga County, and the self-described "eastern gateway to the Finger Lakes."

For this glimpse into distilling history we are indebted to Kihm Winship, a copywriter for a Skaneateles ad agency, who is also a local historian and a pioneering American beer and drinks writer. His research into distilling in and around Skaneateles is recorded in a WordPress blog entry he posted in 2011 called "Skaneateles Whiskey."

Skaneateles is centrally located in New York and is on a major waterway (Skaneateles Lake). The lake feeds an outlet that turns into Skaneateles Creek, which descends through surrounding hills with enough force to power gristmills. The mills, back in the days before electricity and other modern energy sources, used water power to grind the grains that were grown in abundance on surrounding farm fields.

Grain and water—two major ingredients in distilled spirits—were plentiful. "Distilling was, not surprisingly, one of the first industries to accompany the settlement of Skaneateles," Winship writes. And, he points out, distilling, like brewing, had another benefit for rural, farm-based communities like Skaneateles—the spent grain from the process was used to feed cattle, pigs and other livestock.

"Skaneateles whiskey was not sold by the bottle," Winship writes. "If you wanted whiskey, you brought your own gallon jug to the seller, who might be the distiller or a merchant. In 1825, a gallon of whiskey cost 38 cents. And you could buy whiskey by the drink in a tavern or saloon. The earliest Skaneateles distilleries served the immediate area; the later distilleries were huge operations that sold the majority of their product elsewhere, shipping barrels by rail and the Erie Canal."

Winship researched and found tales to tell about roughly a dozen Skaneateles distilleries that operated during the nineteenth century. (Keep in mind, Skaneateles has never been more than a small village of a few hundred or thousand residents). Here's a sampling:

ROBERT & JONAS EARLL DISTILLERY. In 1802, Revolutionary War veteran Robert Earll and his brother Jonas Earll built and operated what appears to have been the area's first distillery, north of the lake and near, but not directly on, Skaneateles Creek. "Using six bushels of wheat a day, the distillery's daily output was 12 gallons of whiskey, which sold for 75 cents a gallon," Winship writes.

WINSTON DAY DISTILLERY. Winston Day appears to have opened his distillery on the creek sometime before 1806. He had been a business partner of Isaac Sherwood, who founded an inn in the village that still stands today, the Sherwood Inn. Celebrated local artist John D. Barrow, Winship discovered, wrote this in 1876 about Winston Day's product: "It was very fiery stuff…but from local patriotism and pride some of the townsmen confessed that they felt it their duty to learn to love it."

EARLL, TALLMAN & CO., AKA EARLLS & TALLMAN DISTILLERY. This distillery was open from 1857 to 1882, according to Winship's research. It was one of several run by family and descendants of Robert Earll and located along Skaneateles Creek near Mottville. "This distillery was by far the largest and most lucrative industry in Skaneateles," Winship writes. In 1882, the distillery was purchased and converted into a paper mill—a fate shared by several of the Skaneateles whiskey makers.

HEZEKIAH EARLL & CO. DISTILLERY AKA HART LOT DISTILLERY AKA EARLL BROTHERS DISTILLERY. This late nineteenth-century distiller was an Earll enterprise with more partners, at Hart Lot north of the village. Its story offers this little Civil War–era economics lesson: "In 1862, to pay for the

Civil War…Congress passed and President Lincoln signed the Tax Act of 1862, which included a tax on all whiskey manufactured after the first day of July 1st," Winship writes. "Every distillery in the country, including the Earll distillery, knowing when the law would go into effect, ran day and night until the last hour of June 30th, accumulating a large stock of whiskey, which at midnight rose in value, netting Hezekiah Earll's sons thousands and thousands of dollars."

Near Skaneateles, Winship found records for another distillery, Carpenter's Distillery, in New Hope (Cayuga County). This one, operating between 1834 and 1875, was one of many businesses using the water power generated by Bear Swamp Creek as it flowed down to Skaneateles Lake. John II. Carpenter bought out a partner in 1844 and added a gristmill and a sawmill. In 1855, the distillery, at the hamlet of New Hope in the town of Niles, used twelve thousand bushels of grain, produced 550 barrels of whiskey and fattened eighty-five hogs with the spent mash.

Winship uses Carpenter's experience to illustrate the rise of the anti-alcohol temperance movement. In this case, he found, Carpenter had "incurred the wrath" of Thurlow Weed Brown (1819–1866), a temperance advocate who edited and published the *Cayuga Chief* in nearby Auburn. Brown frequently wrote of Carpenter and the evils of his distillery, using what Winship calls "impassioned prose." In one case, according to Winship, Brown recorded the death of a man whose corpse was found next to a jug of Carpenter's whiskey.

"Carpenter knew the deceased was under the influence of liquor when at the distillery, and also knew that he had a wife and a large family of children at home," Brown wrote in a piece called "Murder in Niles" in the *Cayuga Chief* on May 21, 1851. "He knew another thing, notwithstanding he swills liquor himself, or his barefaced swearing. He let his victim have his liquor and then over the corpse of the man his whiskey killed swears before God that he thought it would do him good for 'mornings use'!"

Taxes and temperance were the twin killers of the small distilleries in Skaneateles and elsewhere in Upstate New York. "Two factors ended the run of distilleries in Skaneateles. First, safer drinking water and the success of the Temperance movement led to people drinking less whiskey," Winship notes before he lists the accumulating taxes the whiskey makers faced. "Most distillers couldn't wait to get into another line of work."

Small-Batch Distilling Comes Home

It took more than one hundred years for distilling to return to Skaneateles and other small, out-of-the-way towns in the heartland of Upstate New York. We'll get into the story of how the modern resurgence of distilling in Upstate New York came about in a later chapter.

In the meantime, let's look at three of the twenty-first-century distilleries operating in the smaller towns of central New York State. They're the modern equivalent of those small, family-owned distilleries found in Skaneateles and elsewhere in the nineteenth century. These three distilleries embody the spirit of those early spirits makers.

Last Shot Distillery, Skaneateles

In the summer of 2016, distiller Chris Uyehara proudly set a small oak barrel on the bar of the Last Shot Distillery just outside the village of Skaneateles. He inscribed these words on the barrel head: "First barrelled whiskey in Onondaga County since Prohibition."

Uyehara knows his history. He and his partners, building owner John Menapace and John's daughter Kate (the tasting room manager), opened Last Shot in late 2015 on the spot once occupied by the Earll & Kellogg Distillery, on Skaneateles Creek. "We're bringing distilling home to its roots," Uyehara said.

Like many small distillers, Last Shot started with clear or white spirits, including a vodka made from corn and wheat, a moonshine made from corn and a white whiskey called Lightning. (Lightning is both a traditional name for unaged whiskey and the name of a line of sailboats once manufactured on the distillery site.)

Uyehara, a noted local chef, culinary instructor at Syracuse University and a world-class ice carver, also immediately put in motion some aged whiskeys, including a bourbon made from the same mash bill (grains) as the Lightning. That's the whiskey launched in that barrel in the summer of 2016.

Last Shot also makes two spirits distilled from maple syrup, a plentiful local product in the area. One is an unaged White Maple, and the other is Sweet Maple, aged briefly on oak staves and dosed with a shot of syrup at the end for flavor and sweetness.

In 2017, Uyehara introduced a "distiller's reserve," or limited batch whiskey, called Last Shot American Whiskey. It's made with corn, wheat

The first barrel of aged whiskey made in Onondaga County since Prohibition, released in June 2016 at the Last Shot Distillery in Skaneateles. *Author's photo.*

The Lightning Mule, a cocktail made with Lightning (unaged) Whiskey at Last Shot Distillery in Skaneateles. *Author's photo.*

and triticale, a member of the wheat family that tastes a little like rye. The American Whiskey is aged in Last Shot's used bourbon barrels, so it soaks up some of the honey and floral aromas from that spirit.

Here's a cocktail served in the Last Shot tasting room and made with its Lightning Whiskey.

Lightning Mule
From Last Shot Distillery, Skaneateles

1 ½ ounces Last Shot Lightning Whiskey
½ ounce fresh squeezed lemon juice
4 ounces ginger beer
Slice of ginger
Lime wedge

Put whiskey and lemon juice into ice-filled glass, top with ginger beer and stir. Garnish with a slice of ginger and a lime wedge.

Old Home Distillers, Lebanon

Lebanon is a small town that is also the geographic center of New York State. It's close to where the Carvell brothers, Adam and Aaron, grew up.

Both brothers had moved on from their small-town roots in Central New York and found jobs in the drinks and hospitality business elsewhere. Adam Carvell pursued a law degree before deciding it would be more fun to run a bar in Tucson, Arizona. Aaron Carvell had a career in beverage and wine marketing in San Francisco before entering the hospitality industry in New Zealand.

They're still in the drinks business. Only now they're based in Lebanon, where they're running Old Home Distillers, producing whiskey, gin and more. The chance to run the distillery with their mom and dad lured them back home, and Old Home Distillers opened in late 2015.

The idea to open a craft distillery started with Adam Carvell. "I was in the bar business and so I knew small, craft distilling was really picking up," he said. "And I knew it was something we could do here. I knew it was getting big in New York state."

The location they picked is a former "gentleman's horse farm" on Campbell Road, south of Lebanon and close to the little crossroads called

Adam Carvell (*left*) and his brother, Aaron, owners and distillers at Old Home Distillers in Lebanon, New York. *Author's photo.*

The still in action at Old Home Distillers, Lebanon. *Author's photo.*

South Lebanon. The old tack room is the tasting room, and the still and production area is set up in what had been a horse barn.

Their research led them to stories of the small distilleries once set up in the region. A local historian, Stan Roe, shared a story of a nineteenth-century distillery located in a barn not far from the current Old Home site. It used both potatoes and grain to make spirits. A member of the family born in 1852 remembered hearing "his mother tell of men walking down over the hills in the evening for whiskey."

Today, Old Home Distillers has clear spirits, including a corn whiskey, gin and applejack in addition to a flavored maple whiskey and a pumpkin-spiced whiskey, plus two aged bourbons and a single-malt whiskey, made from barley.

The Carvell brothers like to experiment while staying within the spirits-making tradition. They're both beer lovers and dream, for example, of distilling a hoppy India Pale Ale into a new type of spirit.

"We don't want to just make whiskey, gin and vodka," Adam Carvell said. "We want to bring something creative to the process."

Makers of 100 percent barley malt whiskey were relatively rare in the first decade or so of the distilling renaissance in Upstate New York, in part because barley growers and malt houses are few and there is competition for the product with brewers. Here's a cocktail made with Old Home's Single Malt Whiskey (a nod to single-malt scotch):

Burns Night in America
From Old Home Distillers, Lebanon

Absinthe (or absinthe substitute) for rinse
2 ounces Old Home Single Malt Whiskey
½ ounce sweet vermouth
Dash of Angostura bitters

In a chilled cocktail glass, add a few dashes of absinthe, swirling around to coat the glass, and then discard excess. Combine whiskey, vermouth and bitters in a ice-filled shaker; shake and strain into the glass.

Myer Farm Distillers, Ovid

Brothers John and Joe Myer trace their family way back in the history of the town of Ovid, centrally located in Seneca County, the heart of the Finger Lakes.

Some of their ancestors helped found the town in 1789, and one, Andrew Dunlap, is credited with being the first person to plow land in what is today Seneca County. As early as 1810, some members of the family were operating distilleries, making hard liquor out of the grains available in the local countryside: rye, wheat, corn, barley and oats.

Today, John Myer is a farmer, raising many of the same crops in the old-fashioned way, that is, organically. Joe Myer is a former dairy manager, an expert on animal husbandry and a painter, musician and poet.

In 2012, John and Joe opened Myer Farm Distillers in the heart of the Finger Lakes and in the midst of a vibrant winery region. Like the many wineries that sit among the vineyards that supply their grapes, Myer Farm Distillers sits amid the corn and wheat fields that form the base of its spirits. The tasting room is well positioned along the wine trail for those seeking an alternative beverage or two.

Joe Myer in the barrel room at Myer Farm Distillers in Ovid, Seneca County. *Author's photo.*

The Bourbon & Cherry, a cocktail made with John Myer Bourbon Whiskey at Myer Farm Distillers in Ovid. *Author's photo*.

"We had a farm and the farm background," Joe Myer said. "We saw the growth in craft distilling and realized what a perfect opportunity we had to do that together." And, he added about his own decision to return to the farm, "It's hard to get away when it's in your blood."

Myer Farm makes a wide array of spirits, from vodkas (including flavored versions), gins, aged and unaged whiskeys and flavored specialty spirits, including honey, cinnamon and ginger.

The farm is about nine hundred acres, and some 12 to 15 percent of its yield is used by the distillery. The brothers put the philosophy on their website: "At Myer Farm Distillers, we both plant the seed and produce the spirit."

Myer Farm rotates its tasting room cocktail selection frequently. Here are some examples.

Bourbon & Cherry
From Myer Farm Distillers

1 ½ ounces John Myer Bourbon Whiskey
Cherry juice
Bitters, to taste
Orange wedge

Fill a rocks glass with ice. Add whiskey, top with cherry juice. Stir in bitters to taste. Garnish with an orange wedge.

Peach on the Beach
From Myer Farm Distillers

1 ½ ounces Cayuga Gold barrel-aged gin
1 ounce pineapple juice
1 ounce orange juice
1 ounce White Peach Daiquiri Mix (or peach puree)
Maraschino cherry

Shake all ingredients with ice and strain into martini glass. Drop a stemless maraschino cherry into glass.

Drawing of Hustler's Tavern in Lewiston, which some believe was the birthplace of the cocktail. *Lewiston Council on the Arts.*

"Hudson" Mint Julep and Bittered Sling with Rum, two cocktails created by Jori Jayne Emde at Fish & Game. They were inspired by the first definition of the cocktail. *Author's photo.*

The Pineapple Upside Down Cake at Water Street Landing, Lewiston. Blue Chair Bay Rum is bottled in Rochester. *Author's photo.*

Four Grain Bourbon, from Black Button Distilling in Rochester. *Author's photo.*

The Doctor Cocktail, made with Quackenbush Still House Albany Amber Rum, from Albany Distilling Company. *OE Pro Photography for Albany Distilling Company.*

The Nonny Jack Cocktail from the Cocktail Grove at Hudson Valley Distillers, Clermont. *Author's photo.*

Bartender Jeremy Hammill of the Scotch 'n Sirloin in DeWitt mixes a cocktail he created called the Low Bridge at the Erie Canal Museum in Syracuse. *Photo by Dennis Nett.*

An antique cash register behind the bar at the Erie Canal Museum in Syracuse, with a sign poking fun at nineteenth-century temperance activist Carrie Nation. *Author's photo.*

Distiller and co-owner Chris Uyehara at Last Shot Distillery in Skaneateles. *Author's photo.*

A selection of the spirits offered at Old Home Distillers in Lebanon, New York, including corn whiskey, applejack, maple whiskey, malt whiskey and gin. *Author's photo.*

Cocktails at Myer Farm Distillers in Ovid, Seneca County. *Author's photo.*

Tom & Jerry drinks at the Crystal Restaurant in Watertown, where they are a holiday season tradition. *Author's photo.*

Serving Tom & Jerrys from an antique punch bowl at the Crystal Restaurant in Watertown. The drinks are a holiday tradition at the Crystal. *Author's photo.*

The Saratoga Sunrise Cocktail at the Travers Bar at Saratoga Race Course, Saratoga Springs. *Author's photo.*

The Mamie Taylor, named for a renowned Broadway star, was one of the most popular cocktails at the turn of the twentieth century. *Author's photo.*

The Cooperstown Cocktail, a pre-Prohibition drink, as made at the Otesaga Hotel in Cooperstown. *Author's photo.*

The Not a PFD cocktail at the Channelside Restaurant overlooking the St. Lawrence River in Clayton, made with Clayton Distillery Bourbon. *Author's photo.*

Bitters on the bottling line at Fee Brothers in Rochester. The company makes bitters, cordials and other cocktail ingredients. *Author's photo.*

The Flaming Rum Punch, made at the Gould Hotel in Seneca Falls. The town becomes "Bedford Falls" each holiday season in honor of the movie *It's a Wonderful Life*. *Author's photo.*

The Mapple Jack Moonrise, a cocktail at the American Hotel in Sharon Springs. *Author's photo.*

Left: A 1970s poster created by William J. "Bill" Young, who came up with the ad campaign for the Harvey Wallbanger cocktail. *Courtesy of Will Young.*

Below: A neon cocktail sign in the tasting room at Finger Lakes Distilling, in Burdett. *Author's photo.*

The Hot Chai-der cocktail at 1911 Established (Beak and Skiff Orchards), LaFayette. *Author's photo.*

Brian McKenzie, president of Finger Lakes Distilling Company in Burdett. The distillery overlooks Seneca Lake. *Author's photo.*

The White Pike Mojito, at the Finger Lakes Distilling Company. *Author's photo.*

The 585 Cocktail at Black Button Distilling in Rochester, made with the distillery's gin and Bourbon Cream and Fee Brothers Orange Bitters. *Author's photo.*

Spirits produced at Lockhouse Distilling in Buffalo, including a coffee liqueur, Ibisco Bitter, gins and vodkas. *Author's photo.*

The What She's Having cocktail, from Lockhouse Distillery in Buffalo, made with the distillery's Ibisco Bitter. *Author's photo.*

A patron having a tiki cocktail in a coconut at the Ox & Stone bar during the 2016 Rochester Cocktail Revival. *Photo by Katrina Tulloch, NYup.com.*

The Romancing the Stone cocktail in the Turquoise Tiger lounge at the Turning Stone Resort Casino in Verona. *Author's photo.*

Above: Ben Reilley, of the Life of Reilley Distilling Company in Cazenovia, with his Disco Lemonade, New York State's first "cocktail in a can." *Author's photo.*

Left: The New York State Fair Bloody Mary at the Empire Room patio on the state fairgrounds during the 2016 New York State Fair. *Author's photo.*

4

THE "PROFESSOR" AND THE COCKTAIL

THE BARTENDER TURNS PROFESSIONAL

For much of the early to mid-nineteenth century, bars and saloons—and the drinks consumed in them—were on the seedy side of society. You've seen the movies where the cowboy walks into the saloon and gets a quick shot of whiskey or a beer—or both. It was true in the Wild West, but also in parts of the East, like Upstate New York.

"In the 1800s, the saloons thrived because the factory workers, the guys who did dangerous grunt work, had them as the places where they could go to relax—sort of like the modern man-caves," said Dennis Connors, curator of history at the Onondaga Historical Association in Syracuse. In 2014, Connors created an exhibit called "Culture of the Cocktail Hour" at the museum using artifacts from two centuries of Syracuse drinking history.

Drinks author William Grimes, in *Straight Up or On the Rocks*, notes that things were starting to change just before and during the Civil War. It was the time of the creation of a new profession in society: the bartender. Grimes traces the origins of the term to about 1836. At some point during the nineteenth century, the bartender changed from the fellow who slid the beer glass down the bar to someone who might be able to mix you a decent cocktail.

"The mixing of a cocktail was a matter for professionals," Grimes writes. "A man would no sooner shake one up himself than cut his own hair or bake

Tools of the trade for a nineteenth-century bar at the Erie Canal Museum in Syracuse. *Author's photo.*

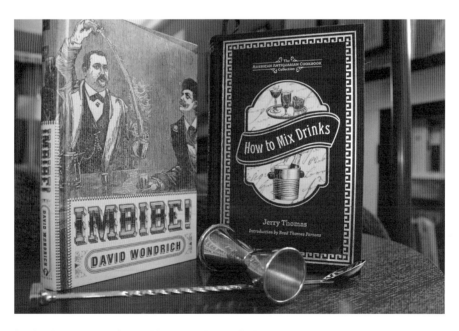

Bar books: a reprint of Jerry Thomas's *How to Mix Drinks* (1862) and *Imbibe!*, the 2007 biography of the celebrated bartender by cocktail historian David Wondrich. *Author's photo.*

his own souffle." And no one did more to change that image than a son of Upstate New York: "The Professor," Jerry Thomas.

He made his name in locales like San Francisco, St. Louis, New Orleans, Chicago and New York City—all the drinking and sporting capitals of nineteenth-century America.

He was the world's first "celebrity" bartender, earning the nickname "The Professor" for his wizardry in concocting creative cocktails. He's credited with inventing (or at least popularizing) many of the classic drinks we know today, along with some long-forgotten libations. He compiled the first book of cocktail recipes ever printed, in 1862.

He was as much a showman as a mixologist, celebrated around the world.

Jerry Thomas was born and raised in Upstate New York. His hometown is Sackets Harbor, located on the often frosty shores of Lake Ontario, just west of Watertown in northern New York. Sackets is an old military town and was the scene of an important naval battle in the War of 1812. A young Ulysses S. Grant was once stationed at the army barracks in Sackets Harbor.

Thomas achieved considerable fame in the mid-1800s—but not for military action or for the other usual paths of that era, like holding political office, writing novels or performing in the theater. His initial renown came from knowing his way around a bar. He wielded a bar spoon, with mixing glasses at hand and bottles of spirits and flavorings at the ready.

During Prohibition, author Herbert Asbury, a frequent (but not always reliable) chronicler of colorful American history, wrote this description of the Professor:

> [He] *was an imposing and lordly figure of a man…portly, sleek and jovial, and yet possessed of immense dignity. A jacket of pure and spotless white encased his great bulk, and a huge and handsome mustache, neatly trimmed in the arresting style called walrus, adorned his lip and lay caressingly athwart his plump and rosy cheeks. He presented an inspiring spectacle as he leaned upon the polished mahogany of his bar, amid the gleam of polished silver and cut glass, and impressively pronounced the immemorial greeting, "What will it be, gentlemen?"*

When Thomas mixed many of his drinks, he put on a show. To make his famous Blue Blazer concoction, for example, Thomas lit whiskey on fire and then mixed or "rolled" it from glass to glass in a pyrotechnic performance behind the bar.

"Like Davy Crockett, Daniel Boone and Buffalo Bill Cody, he was the sort of self-invented, semi-mythic figure that America seemed to spawn in great numbers during its rude adolescence," William Grimes wrote in a 2007 *New York Times* story titled "The Bartender Who Started It All."

Grimes's newspaper account of Thomas's life also marked the publication of a book by fellow cocktail historian David Wondrich. *Imbibe!*, as noted earlier, tells the story of nineteenth-century cocktails and cocktail culture through the lens of Jerry Thomas's life and career. The subtitle expounds upon that journey: "From Absinthe Cocktail to Whiskey Smash, a Salute in Stories and Drinks to 'Professor' Jerry Thomas, Pioneer of the American Bar."

Even a seasoned historian like Wondrich had trouble tracking down details of Thomas's life before he left Sackets Harbor. The future bar star seems to have been born in 1829 or 1830, the son of Jeremiah and Mary Morris Thomas, about whom "we know nothing," Wondrich says. There is evidence he had a brother named George M. Thomas because there are business records showing they ran saloons together at some point.

"His early childhood is a blank," Wondrich writes. "We can deduce that his social class wasn't the highest, but only from his career choices." (Being a barman in the 1800s was not the way to a spot on the Social Register.) According to one obituary, Thomas started his bar career at age sixteen in New Haven, Connecticut. It's not clear how or when he got there.

"New Haven, which was both a seaport and a college town, would have been an excellent place to pick up the rudiments of the [bar] craft," Wondrich writes in *Imbibe!* "In 1846, though, it was a craft still transmitted by long apprenticeship, and his duties in the bar would far more likely have included sweeping, polishing, and carrying than mixing fancy drinks for customers."

He later shipped out as a sailor before returning to bar work, initially in the California Gold Rush. He may also have done some prospecting. His career eventually took him to New York City, where he ran a series of bars before going broke.

His death, in December 1885, merited a news obituary in the *New York Times* under the heading "In and About the City. A Noted Saloon Keeper Dead." The account read, "'Jerry Thomas' as he was familiarly called, was at one time better known to club men and men about town than any other bartender in this city, and he was very popular among all classes."

"Jerry was of an inventive turn of mind and was constantly originating new combinations of drinks," the obituary continued, noting especially his claim to have invented the Tom & Jerry, an egg-based warming winter drink he named for himself. (We'll have more on that drink—and Thomas's dubious claim to be its inventor—later.)

If he didn't invent all the drinks he claimed, he was at least responsible for the first book that collected recipes and techniques. The book had multiple editions, including a noteworthy 1887 revision. It was published under several names, such as *How to Mix Drinks*, *The Bartender's Guide* and, most colorfully, *The Bon Vivant's Companion*.

"So rapturously was *The Bon Vivant's Companion* acclaimed, and so phenomenal its success, that scores of imitations soon appeared, and the book-stalls of the nation groaned beneath the weight of volumes purporting to give directions for the concocting of all sorts of delectable beverages," wrote Asbury in a piece for the *American Mercury* during the height of Prohibition, in December 1927. "But through all this excess of publishing Professor Thomas's work remained steadfastly first in the hearts of his countrymen, everywhere accepted as the production of a Great Master."

Asbury, best known today as the author of *The Gangs of New York*, wrote the introduction that appears on the 1887 edition of Thomas's book. It should be noted that Asbury wrote in extraordinarily purple prose and had little command of facts. He reports, for example, that Thomas was born in New Haven, when that is not the case.

If, during his illustrious career, Jerry Thomas ever used his Upstate boyhood for inspiration in creating drinks, there is no sure evidence. Given his renown, however, you will find various Thomas recipes sprinkled throughout this book.

Scouring his work for Upstate-specific drinks yields a few possibilities. One is called the Knickerbocker, a drink that takes its name from a word used to describe the early Dutch settlers in New York State.

Knickerbocker
From How to Mix Drinks, *by Jerry Thomas*

1 lime or small lemon
3 teaspoons raspberry syrup
1 wineglass Santa Cruz rum
3 dashes Curacao

Squeeze out the juice of the lime or lemon into a small glass; add the rind and the other materials. Fill the glass one-third full of fine ice, shake up well and strain into a cocktail glass. If not sufficiently sweet, add a little more syrup.

Another drink, in the 1887 update, uses Catawba, a popular red wine made from a native North American grape produced in great quantities in Upstate's Finger Lakes and other wine regions in the nineteenth century.

Catawba Cobbler
From The Bartender's Guide, *by Jerry Thomas*

1 teaspoon fine white sugar, dissolved in a little water
1 orange slice, cut into quarters.
Catawba wine
Seasonal berries

Fill a large bar glass half full of shaved ice, sugar and orange and then top with Catawba wine. Ornament the top with berries in season and serve with a straw.

THE LEGACY OF JERRY THOMAS

In the 1920s, Herbert Asbury wrote of Thomas's work, "Even to this day the real adept at manipulating a cocktail-shaker and other such utensils, one who approaches the act of compounding a drink in the proper humbleness of spirit, regards it [Thomas's *The Bon Vivant's Companion*] somewhat as the Modernist regards the Scriptures: as perhaps a trifle out-moded by later discoveries, yet still worthy of all respect and reverence as the foundation of his creed and practice."

In the 1990s and early 2000s, when classic cocktails were "rediscovered" and the art of mixing drinks began its resurgence, the "Scriptures" of Jerry Thomas once again found fame. Many of the mixologists and drinks writers who promoted the return of cocktail culture in America paid homage to Thomas.

In 2003, Robert Hess, who runs the influential cocktail website DrinkBoy. com, wrote a tribute to Thomas. It came on the occasion of a gathering of modern cocktail celebrities at the Plaza Hotel in New York City in which each created a drink from Thomas's catalogue: "Bartenders world-wide owe a debt of gratitude to Jerry Thomas, but unfortunately few modern bartenders know anything about him," Hess wrote. "Jerry Thomas is considered to be the Father of the Cocktail. This is not to say that he invented it, which he did not, but instead that he nurtured it, raised it, and in turn helped to introduce it to the world around him. By profession he was a bartender, and by reputation he was a showman. A combination of skills that we still see in place today behind many bars."

It was Thomas's work, Hess notes, that helped bring the cocktail to the forefront ahead of other mixed drinks. The 1862 book, Hess writes, "was the first recipe book for bartenders, as well as the first book to include recipes for the drink known as the 'cocktail,'" though there were just ten of those in that edition. "Clearly they were just one style, among many other drinks that a bartender was expected to prepare. In later editions of this book, Mr. Thomas would double this count to a full twenty, as well as move it to the front of the book. Clearly the cocktail was building up steam, and Jerry Thomas was right there at the head of the train."

Here's a Jerry Thomas classic, as presented in April 2003 at that modern mixologist gathering at New York City's Plaza Hotel.

Blue Blazer
As Presented by Dale DeGroff

1 ½ ounces Talisker Scotch whiskey, warmed
1 ½ ounce boiling water
¼ ounce simple syrup
Lemon peel

Warm two mugs with hot water. Pour whiskey and boiling water in one mug, ignite the liquid with fire and, while blazing, pour the liquid from one mug to the other four or five times to mix. If done well, this will have the appearance of a continuous stream of fire. Prepare a London dock glass (or Irish coffee glass) with syrup and lemon, and pour the flaming mixture into the glass.

Did drinks like this originate in Upstate New York? Perhaps not, but the man who made them famous certainly did.

A Rochester Bar-Keeper: Patsy McDonough

He was not nearly as famous or revered by modern cocktailians as Jerry Thomas. But Patsy McDonough was another Upstate New York bartender who contributed to the cocktail literature of the late nineteenth century. By the early 1880s, he had already worked at "leading bars" around the country for twenty-five years and was then serving as "head bar-keeper" at Lieder's Hotel Brunswick in Rochester.

That background is included on the title page of *McDonough's Bar-Keeper's Guide and Gentleman's Sideboard Companion*, which appears, from Library of Congress archives, to have been published about 1883.

In his introduction, McDonough writes, "The object of my book is to afford simple and practicable directions for manufacturing all kinds of plain and fancy drinks, that every man may become his own bar-keeper, at home or at the club-room, and at the same time giving to the professional bar-keeper my own extended experience behind the bar."

The recipes, he says, "may be relied upon in every particular as accurate.... Tastes differ in certain cities, and certain drinks, prepared according to the prescriptions in this book, would not perhaps be acceptable all over the country."

Aside from the recipes, McDonough offers a behind-the-scenes glimpse at the life of a bartender of the period:

> *The most unpleasant duties of a bar-keeper is the morning work. Then the bottles, reduced by the demands of the day and night previous, have to be refilled; the glasses used previous to closing, washed; the bar cleaned, and everything put in order for the day....To keep a bar clean and neat during the day, the man in charge should have an abundance of towels—such as fall towels for the front of the bar, hand towels for the rear of the bar, fine linen towels for drying glasses and bottles, and a chamois towel for polishing the glassware....The rear of the bar should be re-arranged at least once a week, and the weekly shifting of the glasses, decanters and bottles of different colors and shapes, will be a constant study for any bar-keeper who has a pride in his work....So, too, the apparel of a first-class bar-keeper....In the winter a neat, fur-trimmed cardigan jacket should be worn; and for summer months, a white duck coat with a white necktie should always be preferred. So, too, the tools necessary for work in a first-class bar, I would mention cork-screws, gimlet, shakers, ice picks, ice shaver, bar spoons, cocktail sieve, lemon knives, lemon squeezers, ice scoop, beer mallet, ale measures, faucets, wine cooler, &c.*

For the drinks, his guide starts with this description: "The Cocktail is a very popular drink. It is most frequently called for in the morning and just before dinner; it is sometimes taken as an appetizer; it is a welcome companion on fishing excursions, and travelers often go provided with it on railroad journeys."

McDonough lists many of the same drinks found in the contemporary editions by Jerry Thomas. It also features some whose names have Upstate New York references. Among them (with the recipes as given):

> BUFFALO PUNCH. *Fill large bar glass with shaved ice, one and one-half table-spoon of bar sugar, one wine-glass of Port Wine, one wine-glass of Brandy, three or four dashes of lime juice; shake well, and add fruit in season. Imbibe through a straw.*

> ROCHESTER PUNCH *for a party of two. One pint imported Champagne, one wine-glass of Brandy, four slices of orange, two slices of pineapple, one table-spoon of powdered sugar to each glass; pour the Brandy on the fruit and sugar them, add the Champagne, which should be taken from the cooler; use a large bar glass; stir with a spoon.*

> ROCHESTER HOT. *One lump of cut loaf sugar, one wine-glass of boiling water, one pony-wine-glass of Irish Whiskey, a small piece of toast, buttered. Use small bar glass*

Another of the drinks found in McDonough's guide is the Tom & Jerry.

TOM & JERRY: A JOYFUL UPSTATE NEW YORK TRADITION

Walk into the Crystal Restaurant in downtown Watertown, New York, any time between Thanksgiving and New Year's Eve, and you're sure to see a large and boisterous crowd at the bar.

They're gathered around a dark blue or black glass bowl and drinking from small milk-white cups with colorful lettering and images. Both the bowl and the glassware are marked with the words "Tom & Jerry."

Yes, it's Tom & Jerry season at the Crystal. This is no cat-and-mouse caper; it's a lasting tribute to a warming winter drink from a bygone age.

The drink itself is a mixture of eggs, spices, rum and brandy that dates back to at least the early 1800s. It's "a rich holiday elixir" in the words of *New York Times* writer Robert Simonson. It is, he continues in an essay in *The*

Essential New York Times Book of Cocktails, "a relative of eggnog that flourished in America in the 19th and early 20th centuries."

There was a time when restaurant bars and taverns across America served Tom & Jerrys in the traditional way that lingers at the Crystal, using a marked punch bowl and mugs. Then fans of the drink brought the tradition home, serving Tom & Jerrys at the holiday gatherings in their parlors.

"The milky broth was once so popular that an ancillary trade in Tom & Jerry punch-bowl sets sprang up," Simonson writes. "You can still spot them in antiques stores, typically emblazoned with the drink's name in Old English type."

Simonson, who grew up in Wisconsin, goes on to observe that this old-fashioned libation "somehow clung to life in Wisconsin and bordering states, while falling into obscurity everywhere else."

Watertown is the major city in Upstate New York's "North Country," a land where winter brings bitter cold temperatures, fierce winds off the Great Lakes and heavy snow, dubbed "lake effect." In other words, it has a lot in common with northern Wisconsin.

It only takes a peek into the Crystal Restaurant during the holidays to see that Watertown is one of the places beyond Wisconsin where the Tom & Jerry clings to life.

"Even if we wanted to stop we couldn't," says Libby Dephtereos, who owns the Crystal with her husband, Peter. "Our customers won't let us."

In the book *A Taste of Upstate New York,* Libby Dephtereos gave this description of the scene at the Crystal during Tom & Jerry season to author Chuck D'Imperio:

> *This place gets packed every day from Thanksgiving to New Year's. The bowl is on the bar and we make each Tom & Jerry to order. Sometimes the girls in the back are making thirty to forty at a time. The magic really does happen back there in the kitchen. Nobody sees the drink being made, and when it comes out to the bar everybody cheers. It is nonstop and it is a madhouse in here. A fun madhouse, though.*

At the bar, the bartender warms your mug with hot water, scoops some batter in from the bowl and adds the liquor. The mix is a family secret, Dephtereos says. "There's not really any measuring to it; everything is just thrown in."

Everything about the Tom & Jerry service at the Crystal evokes old-school tradition. The bowl is an antique that Peter and Libby Dephtereos claimed from the historic former Hotel Woodruff, once located nearby. Most of the glassware dates to the mid-twentieth century. Libby Dephtereos says they find replacements on eBay or from customers. "People bring them in, saying they found these sets in their grandmother's attic," Libby Dephtereos said.

The restaurant itself, on Watertown's historic downtown square, opened in 1925 and hasn't changed much: pressed tin ceiling, wooden booths and floors and a menu of reasonably priced comfort food. Drinks are served from one of those old-time "stand up" bars. There are no seats or stools—never have been. Libby Dephtereos told D'Imperio that the original owner believed if you had so much to drink that you couldn't stand, you should leave.

Peter Dephtereos's family started working there in the 1920s and later bought the restaurant. Libby Dephtereos told D'Imperio that Peter's grandfather, an immigrant from Greece, started the Crystal's Tom & Jerry tradition.

But where, and when, did the Tom & Jerry really get its start? How did it acquire such a fanciful name? This is another of the murky tales that fill spirits and cocktails history. Simonson, in the *New York Times*, writes, "It is frequently (though not definitively) credited to Pierce Egan, the [early nineteenth-century] English chronicler of sports and popular culture. The name, it seems, refers to the lead characters in a book Egan wrote in 1821, *Life in London or the Day and Night Scenes of Jerry Hawthorn, Esq., and His Elegant Friend, Corinthian Tom*.

But there's another story that often pops up (and is just as frequently debunked). It ties the creation of the Tom & Jerry and its name to the bartending celebrity Jerry Thomas, who just happened to be born in Sackets Harbor, not far from Watertown.

Here's the account that appeared in the *New York Times* 1885 obituary of Thomas:

> *Jerry was of an inventive turn of mind and was constantly originating new combinations of drinks, some of which, like the "Tom & Jerry," which he named after himself, became very popular, and, as they could not be patented, were quickly adopted by other saloons for the benefit of their patrons. The drink was first quaffed in 1847, and Mr. Thomas never wearied of telling the story of its first concoction. In repeating it to a friend a few months ago he said: "One day in California a gentleman asked me to give him an egg beaten up in sugar. I prepared the article and*

Tom & Jerry serving bowl and mugs at the Crystal Restaurant, Watertown. *Author's photo.*

then I thought to myself, 'How beautiful the egg and sugar would be with brandy in it!' I ran to the gentleman and said 'If you'll only bear with me for five minutes I'll fix you up a drink that'll do your heartstrings good.' He wasn't at all averse to having his heartstrings improved so back I went and mixed the eggs and sugar, which I had beaten up into a kind of batter, with some brandy. Then I poured some hot water and stirred vigorously. The drink realized my expectations. It was the one thing I had been dreaming of for months. I named the drink after myself. I had two small white mice in those days, one of which I called Tom and the other Jerry. I combined the abbreviations in the drink, as Jeremiah P. Thomas would have sounded rather heavy, and that wouldn't have done for a beverage."

In *Imbibe!*, David Wondrich dismisses the claim. He cites references to the Tom & Jerry drink that appeared long before 1847, including one in a Salem, Massachusetts newspaper from 1827, two or three years before Thomas was born.

At the Crystal, Libby Dephtereos said she'd heard in recent years that a famous bartender named Jerry Thomas might have created the drink long ago, but she had no idea until she was interviewed for this book that he was from the Watertown area.

It seems coincidental, then, that the Tom & Jerry enjoys such a strong reputation so near his birthplace. For Dephtereos, it doesn't matter. "It's just such a great tradition," she said. "We get so many people who come in during the holidays, some from far away, and greet their old friends over a Tom & Jerry or two."

Whether he invented it or not, the Tom & Jerry appears in the first edition of Thomas's cocktail book, *How to Mix Drinks.* Here's his recipe, adapted and annotated for modern tastes by David Wondrich in *Imbibe!*

Tom & Jerry
From How to Mix Drinks *by Jerry Thomas, Adapted by David Wondrich*

Note: Thomas's measurements appear first
(Wondrich's adaptation in parentheses)

12 eggs
1 ½ teaspoons ground cinnamon
½ teaspoon ground cloves
½ teaspoon ground allspice
½ small glass (1 ounce) Jamaica rum
5 pounds (2 pounds) sugar

Use a punch bowl for the mixture: Beat the whites of the eggs to a stiff froth and the yolks until they are as thin as water; mix together and add the spice and rum. Thicken with sugar until the mixture attains the consistency of a light batter. (In his recipe, Thomas notes that "a teaspoonful of cream of tartar, or about as much carbonate of soda as you can get on a dime, will prevent the sugar from settling to the bottom of the mixture.")

To deal out Tom & Jerry to customers: Take a small bar glass and to one tablespoonful of the above mixture, add one wineglass (2 ounces) of brandy and fill the glass with boiling water. Grate a little nutmeg on top. (Thomas notes that some bartenders of his era sometimes substituted a mixture of ½ brandy, ¼ Jamaica rum and ¼ Santa Cruz rum instead of just brandy. "This compound is usually mixed and kept in a bottle, and a wineglass (2 ounces) is used to each tumbler of Tom & Jerry," Thomas notes.)

In *Imbibe!*, Wondrich notes that five pounds of sugar is a "crazy amount" by modern standards. He also notes that hot milk began to replace hot water by the early twentieth century. "It's better that way, although there's a certain austere ruggedness to the water version." He suggests using three pounds of sugar if using water to add body to the finished drink. He also suggests rinsing the serving mugs with boiling water to warm them.

5

THE GILDED AGE

SPORTS, STARS AND CAPITALISTS

Off to the Races: Drinking at Saratoga

They call it the Gilded Age, that period between the Civil War and Prohibition when America matured, gained some measure of prosperity—and refined its drinking habits. Upstate New York was fairly well off in that time, and that was reflected in its cocktail culture.

And no place in Upstate New York did it better than Saratoga Springs.

A day at the races, at a storied horse track like the one in Saratoga Springs, seems to demand a cocktail or two. After all, what's the Kentucky Derby without a mint julep? The drinks at the Saratoga Race Course may not be as globally famous as the julep. But the history is deep.

Early resident Gideon Putnam is credited with taking the edge-of-the-wilderness settlement of the early nineteenth century, located north of Albany and on the edge of the Adirondacks, and turning it into a destination. Its appeal was based largely around its natural mineral springs. (There are twenty-one scattered across town.) Most of the springs are naturally carbonated, and local lore has it that no two taste alike.

In this setting, Putnam built hotels and spas. The Gideon Putnam Hotel, in today's Saratoga Springs State Park, is named for him. The famed racetrack opened in 1864—in the middle of the Civil War.

The link between horse racing, gambling and drinking has always been strong. Saratoga Springs proved to be fertile ground for one of America's earliest examples. The time was ripe in the mid-1800s.

In *Imbibe!*, author David Wondrich's chronicle of nineteenth-century cocktails and biography of bartending celebrity (and Upstate native) Jerry Thomas, a distinction is made between two types of people of that era: The "Victorians" and the "Sports."

The Victorians tended to be hardworking, God-fearing and sober. The Sports, Wondrich writes, "hung around in saloons and gambling halls." They had special interest in two activities, both of which they enjoyed as spectators and wagerers: Horse racing and boxing.

Saratoga Springs, Wondrich writes, was "nineteenth century New York's northern equivalent of the Hamptons, only with gambling." The town boasted a casino as well as a racetrack, and high-stakes card games were common. Those drew Sports from the big city down the Hudson River.

"How pleasant it must have been to catch the morning steamboat and spend the day sipping cooling drinks from the bar and enjoying the breeze as the still largely agricultural Hudson Valley unspooled its vistas before you. A night on the water and next morning you were there."

"As early as 1839," Wondrich continues, "people were remarking on the 'keen blades' who slept in the mornings, antifogmatized immediately with a snort of cognac, smoked and lounged, lounged and smoked, emptied tumblers and popped corks.…By the 1880s, the Cocktail class had more or less taken over the resort."

Clearly, the conditions called for a Saratoga cocktail. In fact, says Wondrich, there were two. One was a Fancy Brandy Cocktail topped with a "squirt" of champagne, which also went by the name Chicago Cocktail.

The other Saratoga Cocktail appears in the 1887 edition of Jerry Thomas's *How to Mix Drinks*.

Saratoga Cocktail
From How to Mix Drinks *(1887), by Jerry Thomas*

2 dashes Angostura bitters
1 pony brandy
1 pony whiskey
1 pony vermouth

Use a small bar glass. Shake up well with two small lumps of ice, strain into a claret glass and serve with a quarter of a slice of lemon.

The Saratoga Cocktail at the Travers Bar at Saratoga Race Course, Saratoga Springs. *Author's photo.*

Note: A pony is 1 ounce. Wondrich says the whiskey should be rye and the vermouth red (sweet). It is, more or less, a Manhattan in which brandy is substituted for half the whiskey.

For good measure, Jerry Thomas included this next Saratoga drink, which, given the egg, may have been intended as a morning "eye opener" for the Sports. Or it may have been what some in Saratoga used to "antifogmatize" themselves.

Saratoga Brace Up
From The Bartender's Guide *(1887), by Jerry Thomas*

1 tablespoon fine white sugar
2 dashes Angostura bitters
4 dashes lemon or lime juice
2 dashes absinthe
1 fresh egg
1 wineglass of brandy
2 or 3 small lumps of ice

Use a large bar glass. Shake up thoroughly, strain into another glass and fill it up with seltzer water.

Today: The Saratoga Sunrise and More

Drinking is still a big part of the Saratoga Springs experience. Today, the town is loaded with bars, restaurants and hotels. It boasts of its mineral springs and spas. It has a popular summertime outdoor music venue—the Saratoga Performing Arts Center.

But it's probably still most famous for the thoroughbred horse track, also called the flat track, officially named the Saratoga Race Course. It opened in 1864 (when the great mixologist Jerry Thomas was still plying his trade). Legends like War Admiral, Whirlaway, Seabiscuit, Secretariat, Funny Cide, American Pharoah and others raced here. The big event each year is the Travers Stakes, Upstate New York's equivalent to a Triple Crown race.

The race course is more than just the track. It's a theme park unto itself. You can watch the races from the grandstand or along the rail or move up in class to the Club House. Many people make use of the spacious grounds to set up picnics of their own, and patronize the eateries, which in recent years have ranged from local food trucks to a branch of Danny Meyer's famous Shake Shack.

The track, operated by the New York Racing Association, also makes it a point to promote New York–produced spirits, beers, ciders and more. On certain race days, tents are set up for brewers, distillers and others to offer samples.

And there are plenty of bars at the track. They include the Fourstardave Sports Bar, the Easy Goer Lounge and others. The Travers Bar, near the Clubhouse Porch, is where we found some modern incarnations of classic Saratoga drinks.

Here's the version of the Saratoga Cocktail, as made by bartender Seth McGuire of food concession company Centerplate at the Travers Bar.

Saratoga Cocktail
As Made at the Saratoga Race Course

1 ½ ounces Hennessy VS Cognac
1 ½ ounces rye whiskey
½ ounce sweet vermouth
3 dashes Angostura bitters

Fill an Old Fashioned glass with ice. Add cognac, rye, vermouth and bitters. Garnish with a twist of lemon.

Today, the signature drink at the track, and the more or less official drink of the Travers Stakes, is not the Saratoga Cocktail of Jerry Thomas's day. It's the Saratoga Sunrise Cocktail. It's a riff off the Tequila Sunrise, and on Travers Day it is served in a souvenir glass.

Why sunrise? Though the post time for the first race on most days is after 1:00 p.m., mornings are especially romantic at Saratoga. Guests may tour the stable areas and even enjoy a breakfast on the Club House porch while watching horses work out on the track.

Saratoga Sunrise
As Made at the Saratoga Race Course

1 ounce Captain Morgan Spiced Rum
1 ounce white rum
Orange juice
Pineapple juice
Grenadine

Fill a highball glass with ice. Add spiced and white rums. Top with equal parts orange and pineapple juice. Drizzle with grenadine (to taste).

Note: This drink is served on Travers Stakes race day in a 12-ounce souvenir glass.

Saratoga Lemonade at the Travers Bar at Saratoga Race Course, Saratoga Springs. *Author's photo.*

The effort to concoct a "signature" drink for the Saratoga Race Course and its premier event has continued into the twenty-first century. In August 2008, the *Albany Times-Union* newspaper held a "Toast to Travers" contest, asking readers to come up with a cocktail to honor the race's namesake, William Travers. The winners, announced in a story by *Times-Union* reporter Steve Barnes, were Tony and Gloria Falco of Guilderland. The drink was dubbed the Travers Cooler and served that year at the track during Travers week.

Travers Cooler
Adapted from Tony and Gloria Falco in the Albany Times-Union

7 mint leaves
2 parts lemon vodka
1 part triple sec
Lemonade, preferably homemade
Lemon wedge or slice for garnish

Muddle 5 mint leaves in bottom of glass. Add ice, vodka, triple sec and lemonade. Shake, pour into rocks glass and garnish with remaining 2 mint leaves and lemon.

Note: The Travers Club at the Saratoga Race Course serves a variation on this called Saratoga Lemonade.

A COCKTAIL STAR: THE MAMIE TAYLOR

The year was 1899. The place was Ontario Beach, on the Lake Ontario shoreline, just outside Rochester. A star was present. A drink was born.

Think of the intersection between entertainment and celebrity on one side and the rise of a cocktail on the other and you might think of something like the Cosmopolitan. That was the drink launched into the mixology stratosphere by the TV show *Sex and the City* at the turn of the twenty-first century.

One hundred years earlier, without the benefit of TV or Internet hype, another drink inspired by celebrity caught the imagination of drinkers everywhere: the Mamie Taylor.

The Mamie Taylor cocktail was named for turn-of-the-century Broadway star Mamie Taylor, featured in the book *Vintage Spirits and Forgotten Cocktails*, by Ted Haigh. *Author's photo.*

Mamie Taylor was a star—a big one. She was a prima donna of Broadway shows and light operas. The story of how she came to inspire a drink is told in this report from the *Syracuse Post-Standard* on March 7, 1902:

> *It was while Miss Taylor was the prima donna of an opera company playing at Ontario Beach, near Rochester, in 1899…that she was asked with a number of other members of the company to go out sailing on the lake. As the day was hot and the breeze rather strong, the party returned after*

a few hours longing for some cooling refreshments. When Miss Taylor was asked what she would have she expressed the wish for a long but not strong drink....On tasting it Miss Taylor found it much to her liking, but asked to have the flavor softened with a piece of lemon peel. When this was done the new combination drink was declared a complete success. Bystanders had been watching the proceedings and noticing the evident enjoyment with which Miss Taylor and a few of her friends relished the new drink they finally asked the hotel keeper what drink it was that was being served to them and without hesitation the hotel man replied "a Mamie Taylor" and the name seemed to meet with instantaneous favour and has become famous all over the country.

The drink itself was a simple mix of scotch and lime juice, poured into an ice-filled glass and topped with ginger ale. It was an early version of a highball.

From the shores of Lake Ontario, the Mamie Taylor—attributed in most accounts to a hotel bartender named Bill Sterritt—quickly made the jump to national fame. The big boost apparently came when it was served to much acclaim at the Republican National Convention in Philadelphia in 1900.

In *Vintage Spirits and Forgotten Cocktails*, drinks writer and historian Ted Haigh writes, "At the dawn of the twentieth century the Mamie Taylor stood as proud as the Statue of Liberty." He cites a July 1900 *New York Daily News* report, "The latest hit on these hot days is a nice cool 'Mamie Taylor.'"

"Thousands were consumed that year," Haigh writes. "They were advertised by name in newspaper ads. Poems were written about the drink, jokes were told and articles were written using Mamie to illustrate au courant sophistication."

The Mamie Taylor's fame was enormous, but it didn't last.

"By 1904," Haigh writes, "the *Washington Post* cited a bartender grumping, 'Well, that's the first call for her we've had in nearly three years,' as he mixed the drink." The same fleeting fame apparently struck Mamie Taylor, the actress/singer, Haigh says.

Mamie Taylor—whether you mean the drink or the person—"has virtually no name recognition today," Haigh noted in the 2009 revised edition of his book. But short-lived fame is better than none.

"Although it remained a posh drink of the privileged class for a few more years, to the common man, the Mamie Taylor was synonymous with 'swank refreshment' until 1920 and Prohibition," Haigh writes. Yet it did appear in bar books through the 1950s.

Forgotten or Not:
Making a Mamie Taylor

As noted, the Mamie Taylor is a highball—a tall drink of spirits and lime served over ice with a mixer. It's quite similar to a drink that has found resurgent popularity in recent years—the Moscow Mule. That one—vodka, lime and ginger ale or ginger beer—is typically served in a small copper mug instead of a highball glass. You may also note its similarity to the Dark 'n Stormy, which substitutes Gosling's Black Seal Rum for scotch or vodka.

"The Mamie Taylor is a drink that has had wide influence, even if people don't know it now," Haigh said in an interview with the *Syracuse Post-Standard* in 2009. "It's the drink I use on people who profess not to like Scotch."

In *The Stork Club Bar Book* (1934), a classic of New York City's golden age of cocktails, author Lucius Beebe gives the recipe using a slice of lemon but no lime. In *The Old Waldorf-Astoria Bar Book* (1935), another New York City gem, author A.S. Crockett offers up "the juice one half lime, one jigger Scotch Whiskey and one bottle imported ginger ale." In the more modern *The Joy of Mixology* (2003), by Gary Regan, the drink is made with one lemon wedge, two ounces scotch and three ounces ginger ale.

Here's the version given by Ted Haigh:

Mamie Taylor
From Ted Haigh in Vintage Spirits and Forgotten Cocktails

2 ounces scotch
¾ ounce freshly squeezed lime juice
Spicy ginger ale or ginger beer (Haigh recommends Blenheim's no. 3 ginger ale)

Pour the scotch and lime juice into an ice-filled 8-ounce highball glass and fill with ginger ale. Stir and garnish with a lime wedge.

Note: Gary Regan, drinks writer and master mixologist, observes that many of the classic recipes, like Haigh's, omit the lemon twist garnish that Taylor herself called for according to the early newspaper accounts of the drink's creation. "Why this recipe doesn't call for a lemon twist garnish, when the newspaper quote plainly states that Ms. Taylor demanded one, I've no idea, but I can't find a recipe anywhere that includes such a thing," Regan says. "Your call. I add a lemon twist."

Cooperstown: Cocktails on the Diamond

Baseball has no official cocktail (unless you consider beer a cocktail). But America's pastime does share something in common with the mixed drink: its origins are hazy, leading to several myths and legends.

Just as some of the myths regarding the cocktail have Upstate New York connections, so too does the story of baseball. Abner Doubleday, it is said, invented the game in the village of Cooperstown in 1839. That led to the founding, one hundred years later, of what is now the National Baseball Hall of Fame and Museum in the heart of the beautiful village on Otsego Lake.

Never mind that most experts now debunk the Doubleday baseball tale. Consider this coincidence: Cooperstown was founded and named for the father of author James Fenimore Cooper. The novelist grew up in Cooperstown, and as we noted in chapter 1, he is a key figure in some of the early founding myths of the cocktail.

And while there is no baseball cocktail, there is one named for Cooperstown. Its connection to Cooperstown, the village, is not clear.

It appears in a 1917 book called *The Ideal Bartender* by a pre-Prohibition mixologist named Tom Bullock. Bullock was a well-known bartender in his day, working in such cities as Cincinnati, Chicago, Louisville and, most notably, St. Louis, where he mixed drinks at the St. Louis Country Club. The drink also has a brief mention in the 1935 edition of the *Old Waldorf-Astoria Bar Book*, where it is simply described as a "Bronx, with fresh mint," the recipe for the Bronx Cocktail having been given earlier.

The Cooperstown Cocktail also made its way into the revised version of *The Waldorf-Astoria Bar Book* in 2016. Author Frank Caiafa, manager of the modern Peacock Alley bar in the Waldorf, researched and adapted many of the old recipes. He notes, "The Old Bar entry for the Cooperstown is dedicated to one Craig Wadsworth and the 'young sportsmen' from 'the richest and prettiest town up-State.'"

That may be how it got its name.

The Cooperstown Cocktail is not exactly popular today. Even in Cooperstown, it doesn't seem to feature on drinks lists. We stopped in at one of the village's grandest venues, the Otesaga Hotel on the shore of Otsego Lake, and asked beverage manager Chad Douglass to make one for us. He adapted the classic version introduced by Tom Bullock.

Cooperstown Cocktail
From The Ideal Bartender *(1917), by Tom Bullock*

One jigger (1 ½ ounces) of Sir Robert Burnette's Old Tom Gin (see note)
½ pony (½ ounce) of Italian vermouth
Six leaves of fresh mint

Use large bar glass. Fill with lump ice. Shake ingredients together. Strain and serve in cocktail glass

Note: Douglass at the Otesaga Hotel substitutes locally produced Fenimore Gin from the nearby Cooperstown Distillery. "I try to make all our cocktails as local as I can," Douglass said. Old Tom, by the way, was a sweeter version of gin that gave way to the more common London Dry style of gin in the twentieth century.

Here's a modern version in the revised *Waldorf-Astoria Bar Book*, by Frank Caiafa.

Cooperstown Cocktail
From The Waldorf-Astoria Bar Book *(2016)*

1 ½ ounces Tanqueray London Dry gin
½ ounce Dolin de Chambery sweet vermouth
½ ounce Dolin de Chambery dry vermouth
1 ounce fresh orange juice
1 dash Regan's Orange Bitters No. 6 (optional)
12 fresh mint leaves

Add all ingredients to mixing glass. Add ice and shake well. Fine-strain into a chilled cocktail glass. No garnish.

Cooperstown Distillery is just a few blocks from the Otesaga Hotel and also near the Baseball Hall of Fame. Its spirits include Sam Smith's Boatyard Rum, Glimmerglass Vodka and several variations on bourbon and American whiskey. In 2016, it introduced Spitball, a cinnamon-flavored slightly sweet whiskey that "packs a powerful punch of heat," the distillery says. It is fierier than the leading national brand, Fireball. Here's a cocktail featuring Spitball and one of Cooperstown's bourbons.

Spicy Manhattan
From Cooperstown Distillery

2 ounces Spitball Whiskey
2 ounces Beanball Bourbon
Splash of sweet vermouth

Combine and stir over ice. Strain into a chilled glass and garnish with a cherry and orange twist.

BIG BUSINESS AND A LITTLE FRAUD

Taxes and temperance, as we've seen, spelled the end for many of Upstate New York's small-scale nineteenth-century distillers, in such out-of-the-way locations as Skaneateles in the Finger Lakes.

Yet as the century wore on and the distilling companies dwindled in number, they also grew larger. It was the Gilded Age, the era of capitalism with a capital *C*. Big distillers were part of the picture, and Upstate New York was no exception.

In 1884, E.N. Cook & Co. Distillers of Buffalo published a book called *Scientific Bar Keeping: A Collection of Recipes and New Fancy Mixed Drinks*. The title page includes this description of its operation:

> *Our distillery No. 1 occupies the entire block bounded by Spring, Champlin, Tousey and Mortimer Streets, and No. 2 is located on the block bounded by Pratt, William and Spring Streets. They are the largest distilleries in the State, No. 1 having a capacity of 2,000 bushels, and No. 2, 1,600 bushels, daily. Our regular products are Rye, Bourbon and Malt Whiskies, and Gin distilled by the same process as in Holland, and is known as E..N. Cook & Co.'s Holland Gin. We are also the distillers of the famous* GOLDEN GRAIN WHISKY.

Cook's size was matched by its bravado: "It is almost superfluous to dwell upon the merits of our productions," the company declared in the book's introduction. "The fact that our goods are sold by the largest Wholesale Liquor Dealers in the trade, and have been accepted, and now are used, by all leading hotels, saloons, etc., everywhere, speaks for itself. We distill our

Antique bottle from E.N. Cook Distilling Co. of Buffalo, photographed at Lockhouse Distilling in Buffalo. *Sara Heidinger Photography.*

whiskies from the best selected grain, and the reports of chemists who have analyzed them evidence their purity."

Cook was among just a handful of distillers operating in Upstate New York around the end of the nineteenth century and the dawn of the twentieth, up to Prohibition. The exact number is not clear, with conflicting accounts. (The count is also confused by the use of the term "rectifier," which in some cases meant a company that simply blended, modified and/or repackaged spirits distilled elsewhere.)

These big distillers were the survivors of the days of smaller scale distilling. One other big Upstate distiller of the late 1800s—Columbia Distilling Company—had started in the small Finger Lakes town of Waterloo in 1838. By the turn of the century, it had offices in Albany.

In an article for the Buffalo Architecture and History site, buffaloah.com, local historian and collector Peter Jablonski wrote about the effect of taxes on the distilling business: "The government was taxing 90 cents per gallon

Antique whiskey bottle for Century Club Whiskey at the Onondaga Historical Association Museum, Syracuse. *Photo by David Lassman, syracuse.com.*

and forcing companies to manufacture 80% of their capacity whether for a loss or profit. This necessitated many of them to shut down. Many of the vacated buildings became warehouses. Because Buffalo was a grain terminus, the two largest in the state were located here."

One of those, Jablonski says, traced its origins to what may have been Buffalo's earliest distillery, "built in a little frame shanty on the Seneca plank road, about five years after the opening of the Erie Canal in 1826." By the 1840s, the property was operated by Thomas Clark, who built a large malt house. In 1862, Jablonski notes, when "Congress first passed a law imposing tax on distilled spirit, Mr. Clark was producing 1,000 gallons per day." The name of his business was the Old Red Jacket Distillery, named after a Seneca Indian chief.

The other distillery was the one that became E.N. Cook. It was built by George Truscott at the corner of Pratt and William Streets just before the Civil War. It had several other owners before being shut down in 1883, when, Jablonski writes, "the government took possession under a warrant for failure to maintain the stipulated eighty percent of the total capacity of the distillery." It was then purchased and operated by E.N. Cook. Records show the distillery paid $30,000 a month in taxes.

"In a word," Jablonski writes, "the distilling industry of Buffalo and Western New York was comprised within a single name, that of E. N. Cook and Company. The rest of the dealers were whiskey wholesalers."

Making or selling whiskey—while keeping the tax man and the temperance activists at bay—seemed to require a special breed of entrepreneur in the decades before Prohibition. The stories of three such men in Upstate New York—associated with the Cook, Columbia and Duffy distilleries—are told in a series of articles written by amateur historian Jack Sullivan in a blog he calls "Those Pre-Prohibition Whiskey Men!"

In Buffalo, he focuses on Gustav Fleischmann, who was Edward Cook's partner in E.N. Cook & Co. Fleischmann was the younger brother of Max and Charles Fleischmann, who founded a bread yeast manufacturing company in Cincinnati that still exists as a brand today. The Fleischmann-Cook partnership started with the distillation of rum, possibly for the first time in New York State since the closing of the Albany rum business in the early 1800s.

Gustav Fleischmann bought out Cook in 1893, renamed it Buffalo Distilling Company and continued to make gins, whiskeys and more, headed by the flagship Golden Grain Whiskey. According to Sullivan, Fleischmann was a good marketing man fond of giveaways, including a celluloid pocket charm. One had an inscription that read "This charm if carried in the pocket of a person who drinks Golden Grain Whiskey prevent(s) Bald Heads, Hard Work, Love, Warts on the Nose, Bicycle Fact, Dark Brown Taste, War Craze, Swelled Head, Delirium Tremens, Unhappy Marriages, Insanity and Punctured Tires. Avoid Substitutes." Buffalo Distilling lasted until the advent of Prohibition.

Then there was Charles Tracey of Albany. He had a distinguished career, including service in the army of the pope in the mid-1800s, after which he was given the title "Chevalier," Sullivan writes. In America, Tracey also earned the titles colonel and later, general. Tracey was an adviser to four New York governors, including one who also served as president, Grover Cleveland, and served four terms in the House of Representatives.

He also found time to succeed his father, John, in running the family business, Columbia Distilling. Letterheads and business cards indicate Columbia had its origins in Waterloo, a small town at the north end of the Finger Lakes between Syracuse and Rochester, and was founded

A late nineteenth-century ad touting the health benefits of Duffy's Malt Whiskey, made in Rochester. *New York Public Library.*

in 1838. It's likely the company maintained its distillery, or rectifier, in Waterloo and kept its bonded warehouses there. Its brands included Beaver Rye, Carlisle Rye, Columbia Rye, Dongan Club, Evermore and Seneca Chief.

The company eventually established headquarters offices in Albany, but it's not clear whether spirits were made there, Sullivan writes. In 1900, Tracey sold Columbia to a distillery combine called the New York and Kentucky Company, headed by Walter B. Duffy, who owned the Duffy Malt Whiskey Company in Rochester. Tracey remained on the combine's board. It, too, closed with Prohibition.

And now we come to Walter B. Duffy of Rochester. He was probably the wiliest of all the Upstate pre-Prohibition "whiskey men." Consider the title of Sullivan's article on him: "How Mr. Duffy Outwitted Uncle Sam—and Got Rich," or another, from a blog called Sipp'n Corn, "False Advertising and the Legacy of Duffy's Pure Malt Whiskey."

Mr. Duffy seems to have been a whiskey distiller and a snake oil salesman.

Duffy was born in Canada in 1840 and moved with his family to Rochester a few years later. He served in the Union army during the Civil War and later joined his father's cider refining business, which he greatly expanded. "In 1881 the Rochester directory lists Duffy as a distiller and rectifier of alcohol, 'French spirits,' and malt, wheat, rye and bourbon whiskies," Sullivan writes. Duffy also opened a second distillery in Baltimore.

In no time, Duffy began pitching the medicinal qualities of his products, according to Sullivan and to Brian Haara, whose Sipp'n Corn blog traces the story of "bourbon as told through the rich history of American lawsuits." Claiming health benefits was not uncommon, Sullivan writes, but Duffy took it to a new level:

> *The 1880s were a time when patent medicines began their meteoric rise in popularity by aggressive advertising and other ploys. Many whiskey makers began to advertise their wares as being "for medicinal use" without being specific as to the ills they were meant to remedy. Duffy took a different approach. He decided to straddle the divide between selling the 15 cent saloon shot and hawking his booze as a cure for specific diseases. Thus about 1885—the year it was registered with the government—was born the Celebrated Duffy's Malt Whiskey, which he advertised as the "greatest known heart tonic."*

In his blog, Haara adds, "By the early 1880s, Duffy was advertising his Duffy's Malt Whiskey not only as a tonic that 'Makes the Weak Strong,' but also as a cure for all sorts of diseases. Consumption, influenza, bronchitis, indigestion, and practically old age itself were claimed to be no match for Duffy's Malt Whiskey."

Despite all that, Duffy ran into financial trouble and declared bankruptcy in 1886. "A complicated financial deal had failed, one of Duffy's partners was headed for Honduras, and he himself was lying low," Sullivan reports.

But Duffy rebounded—and in a big way. He continued to make dubious health claims about his whiskey. "The success of Duffy's Malt Whiskey as a cure almost certainly helped solve Walter's bankruptcy woes," Sullivan writes. "His claim that 'malt whiskey' really was medicine even convinced some Temperance advocates. Duffy backed up his fiction by concocting a story that his remedy was made from 'a formula worked out fifty years ago by one of the World's Greatest Chemists.' The distiller featured a trade mark of a bearded scientist who apparently had discovered this wonder liquid."

"To validate his therapeutic claims," Sullivan adds, "he gave away glass medicine spoons rather than shot glasses." The stage was set for Duffy to perpetrate his biggest outrage. Recall that whiskey in those days was taxed at ninety cents per gallon. In 1898, with the Spanish American War raging, Congress looked for other ways to generate revenue and approved a special tax on patent medicines. That tax amounted to two cents per bottle, Sullivan writes.

On July 5, 1898, "the Commissioner of Internal Revenue, N.B. Scott, wrote to the local collector of revenues in Rochester ruling that: 'Duffy's Pure Malt Whiskey, is by being advertised as a cure for consumption, dyspepsia, malaria, etc., liable to a stamp tax as a medicinal article.'"

Let's do some quick math. At ninety cents a gallon, whiskey would have been taxed at eighteen cents for a standard bottle—a fifth of a gallon. But as a medicine, Duffy's whiskey was now being taxed at two cents per bottle.

"We can imagine Commissioner Scott laughing about sticking it to Duffy as he signed the order [requiring Duffy's to be taxed as medicine]," Sullivan writes. "In reality, the Feds did Walter two enormous, if unintended, favors. Estimates are that before it was repealed after the war, the stamp tax cost him about $40,000, not an inconsiderable sum. At the same time, however, it exempted him from hundreds of thousands in federal and state liquor taxes and allowed him to advertise with some legitimacy as 'the only whiskey recognized by the Government as medicine'—a claim that turned out to be worth millions."

But Duffy's success also made him a target. The famous muckraking journalist Samuel Hopkins Adams exposed the phoniness of Duffy's ads claiming health benefits, part of a series of articles in *Collier's Magazine* that helped lead to the passage of the federal Pure Food and Drug Act in 1906. "Nevertheless," Sullivan notes, "Adams' revelations failed to dampen sales."

In 1907, Sullivan says, the first head of the Food and Drug Administration, Dr. Harvey W. Wylie, "took aim at Duffy—and ended frustrated with Washington bureaucratic foot-dragging."

"I stated that Duffy's Malt Whisky was one of the most gigantic frauds of the age and a flagrant violation of the law," Wylie said, "and that there was no necessity that we delay at all in the matter." Despite years of effort, Wylie failed to get a federal case lodged against Duffy.

The state of New York had better luck. In 1905, Patrick W. Cullinan, the New York commissioner of excise, "went to court claiming that Duffy's was nothing more than sweetened whiskey and subject to state liquor taxes," Sullivan writes. "The company countered with eleven physicians, four of them members of the Rochester Health Department, who swore their belief that the whiskey contained drugs that made it real medicine."

The New York Supreme Court sided with Cullinan and ruled that Duffy's should now be taxed as liquor. "This proved to be only a slight setback to Duffy: the money continued to roll in," Sullivan writes. "As a result of this soaring success, the formerly bankrupt Walter Duffy now was on his way to becoming a multimillionaire."

Duffy died rich in 1911. And yet his success spurred the forces that eventually killed the business. His false advertising sparked the reporting of muckrakers like Adams, which led to the Pure Food and Drug Act. Over time, that law controlled some of the outlandish claims and business practices of the era. Among the act's many achievements, it ended the practice of "rectifiers," who passed off flavored rot-gut as real aged whiskey and established such definitions as "straight" and "blended" whiskey.

So now, thanks to Duffy, the era when whiskey could be called a cure-all was at an end. Soon, whiskey itself would be outlawed.

6

PROHIBITION

THE DRY (AND NOT-SO-DRY) YEARS

Bootleggers and Speakeasies

"With Prohibition, the golden age of the cocktail came to a dead stop," William Grimes writes in *Straight Up or On the Rocks: The Story of the American Cocktail*. "It was too good to last, and Americans seemed to recognize the fact. The saloon went out with barely a whimper: the night of Jan. 16 1920, saw a resigned, peaceful America drift quietly into a theoretically cocktail-free era."

Theoretically is the key word here. In Upstate New York, as in the rest of the United States, the making and drinking of alcoholic beverages didn't stop just because the government said they should. New York State was always less friendly to Prohibition than other states anyway. Two of its Prohibition-era governors ran for president on platforms that favored repeal: Al Smith, who lost in 1928, and Franklin Delano Roosevelt, who ran and won in 1932 and whose new administration coincided with the end of Prohibition.

As a border state, New York was also the scene of considerable bootlegging, one of the most notorious activities of the Prohibition era (or romantic, depending on your point of view). New York City and Long Island obviously were great ports of entry for illegal hooch. But don't ignore that long border with Canada that stretches from Plattsburgh, just south of Montreal, west along the St. Lawrence River and Lake Ontario before turning south along the Niagara River and Lake Erie.

Badges, handcuffs and billy clubs used by authorities to enforce Prohibition, at the Onondaga Historical Association Museum, Syracuse. *Photo by David Lassman, syracuse.com.*

They weren't always running rum. But they were running alcohol.

Not surprisingly, the Thousand Islands, on the United States–Canadian border where the St. Lawrence and Lake Ontario meet, was a hotbed for bootleggers. The islands, sprinkled along both sides of the border, offered perfect cover for rumrunning between Canadian towns like Kingston and Gananoque and American towns like Clayton and Alexandria Bay.

In 2014, Clayton resident Nancy Bond wrote an article for *Thousand Islands Life* about the era of bootlegging in that region. She recalled that "several people who live in Clayton are descendants of those daring young men who made sure that there was whiskey to be found, if you knew where to look. Of course, it was illegal and carried heavy fines if you were caught, but it also was very hard and dangerous work, and bootleggers were considered heroes by many people. Their lives were romanticized, and I believe more upstanding citizens were inclined to sympathize with the bootleggers, rather than the law."

Bond also told this personal story:

My husband Leo's family lived on a small farm on Grenadier Island near Cape Vincent, in the early thirties....His Father, Frank, told of one snowy winter day when a big Packard came across the ice from Kingston [in Ontario] and was trying to cross the Island to make it to the American shore. They got stuck in a huge snow bank and came knocking late one night asking for help to get under headway again. Frank got the big team of work horse[s], and pulled them out of the drifts and helped them on their way. They were very grateful and presented him with a bottle of good whiskey to repay the favor. They told him it was their last run. They were nervous about the law catching them and were going to get out of the business. They went on their way, but a little later there was a big explosion. It seems the law did catch up with them and apparently had shot the car, exploding the gas tank or the Whiskey or both. It truly was their last run!

At a site called northcountryfolklore.org, affiliated with a group called Traditional Arts of Upstate New York, a Clayton boat captain named Lawrence Balcom recounted this tale of his youth:

During Prohibition, it was also the Depression, but along the river here, we never knew that, 'cause almost everybody was a bootlegger. My first experience, I was nine years old, and my neighbor was ten, and my grandfather had built a little fourteen foot sharpie, which is just a flat bottom boat with a bow on it. We would go around town and we'd collect cardboard boxes. We'd take these boxes to the bathing suit factory and they would give us a nickel apiece for them. And we'd save up until we had fifty cents, sometimes a dollar, not very often a dollar. And on Saturday we'd row over to Gananoque and we'd each buy a pint of whiskey. It was twenty five cents a pint. At that time there was a whole row of small boathouses in Gananoque and we'd row over there, and whoever was selling the whiskey at the time had a shamrock, and whichever boathouse that shamrock was hangin' over, that's the one you went in and bought your whiskey. We'd row back to Clayton and we'd take the whiskey up to a fella here named Bill Bartlett and he would give us 100 per cent profit on our money. Fifty cents a pint for it. So, if we made a dollar that day, boy, we made a lot of money!....Now, we had a ferry running from Gananoque to Clayton, and every time they'd land in Clayton the customs officers would go aboard and they'd search and normally they'd find eight or ten bottles of whiskey every trip. Some people would take the corks out of the bottles and drop them over the side. Now, because of the specific density of the alcohol, the bottles would float for awhile, so when the ferry left, we would dive down and put the bottles up on the pier. Then, after dark, we'd go down and sneak it up to Bill and sell it to him. So, I guess we were junior bootleggers!

Along with bootleggers, the Prohibition era was also noted for its speakeasies, the illegal drinking joints of the day. "The City of Buffalo, like many other American cities, had its share of smuggling stories and speakeasies, perhaps more than its share," author and historian Stephen R. Powell recounts in his book *Rushing the Growler: A History of Brewing in Buffalo.*

According to Buffalo mayor F.X. Schwab in his 1922 annual state of the city address there were 8,000 "soft drink" places where illegal liquor and beer could be obtained and consumed. With the city's unique geographic position along the Canadian border, the temptation for smuggling was great. Unlike the rest of the country Buffalonians could cross the border to Canada, where liquor was still legal, for a drink if they wanted to. If they were brave and clever they could smuggle some back home with them.

In Syracuse, one of the most notorious speakeasies was located in the heart of downtown, in a relatively nondescript building next to the First Baptist Church, according to Dennis Connors, curator of history at the Onondaga Historical Association. He collected stories and artifacts of the era as part of a 2014 OHA exhibit called "Culture of the Cocktail Hour," tracing the history of drinking in Syracuse.

One of Connors's favorite stories concerns this downtown speakeasy, which catered to a well-heeled and no doubt powerful clientele and was therefore difficult for the authorities to shut down. But there was an unexpected raid one night, and the operator did his best to hide the liquor by throwing it out a rear window—onto a back roof of the Baptist church.

"The pastor (Reverend Dr. Clausen) was furious," Connors said. "He was a Prohibition supporter, and these people had the nerve to operate next to his church, and dump their liquor on his property."

Where there was bootlegging, of course, there were also gangsters. Albany boasted connections to some of the most famous gangsters of the era, including Dutch Schultz and his arch-rival, Jack "Legs" Diamond.

Replica of a Prohibition-era speakeasy at the Onondaga Historical Association museum, Syracuse. *Photo by David Lassman, syracuse.com.*

Diamond, who had moved his operation from New York City to the state capital during Prohibition, was shot to death in 1931 in an Albany rooming house.

In his illustrated history, *Albany: Capital City on the Hudson*, author John J. McEneny notes that the state capital was a "crossroads" of the bootleg liquor trade and a place where people liked to drink. "And drink they did," McEneny writes, "Smuggled scotch from Canada, applejack from nearby farms in Albany County and rural areas beyond, and bathtub gin made by local people in exactly the way the name implies."

McEneny also does his best to name-check some of the Albany region's speakeasies and illicit drinks joints. Some, like the one in Syracuse, seemed to be hiding in plain sight. "Ames O'Brien's Parody Club was on Hudson, next to the firehouse," he writes, "not far from Foggy Farrell's on Green Street and the famous 'Big Charley' Van Zandt at Green and Division." Illegal breweries and distilleries also "cropped up everywhere," McEneny says. "Worst among the offenders were the druggists of the city, who dispensed 'medicinal alcohol' at an alarming rate, both over the counter and out the back door."

McEneny also cites what some people called the "most insidious" feature of Prohibition. It "introduced women to the bars. Unlike their predecessors [pre-Prohibition saloons], the speakeasies were used for courtship and dating."

Dennis Connors found the same thing while curating the drinking history exhibit at Syracuse's Onondaga Historical Association:

Through much of the 19th century, drinking at bars, saloons and gentleman's clubs was a predominantly, almost exclusively, a male activity. It was Prohibition, in the 1920s, that really changed things....Because Prohibition forced drinking underground, it was easier for women to participate. They could do something hidden away that they hadn't been able to do out in the open....It really was the glory days of the cocktail because the liquor was so bad, made in bathtubs and so forth, that they learned to mix in ingredients that really masked those flavors....So you had women, mixed drinks and a lot of creativity at that time.

THOUSAND ISLANDS TODAY:
LEGAL LIQUOR AND COCKTAILS

The bootleggers and illicit hooch makers no longer add character to the Thousand Islands. Today, it's the entirely legal cocktail bars and craft distilleries who bring the local flavor.

Clayton Distillery opened in 2013, and owner Mike Aubertine makes vodka, gin, bourbon, flavored whiskeys and liqueurs and a popular line of flavored and unflavored moonshines. The Lemonade Moonshine is the most popular, Auburtine says. (Perhaps it's the slightly illegal sound of *moonshine* that adds to the allure.) Most of the spirits are distilled from New York–grown corn.

Clayton sits right on the St. Lawrence River, making it an attractive destination for summer tourists, although it seems slightly less touristy than its nearby neighbor, Alexandria Bay, home of the famous Boldt Castle. Clayton has the Antique Boat Museum and is said to be the birthplace of Thousand Island salad dressing.

Aubertine, who is also an architect in nearby Watertown, chose Clayton for his distillery because, he believes, "It's becoming a little more progressive—a little more upscale—and has lots of great restaurants and bars."

The tasting room is a hopping place, with many signature cocktails available.

Owner Mike Aubertine at the Clayton Distillery in Clayton. *Author's photo.*

The Admiral's Lemonade cocktail, at Clayton Distillery, made with the distillery's berry vodka and two flavored liqueurs. *Author's photo.*

Admiral's Raspberry Lemonade
From Clayton Distillery

¾ ounce Clayton Distillery Admiral's Berry-Flavored Vodka
¼ ounce Clayton Distillery Limoncello
3 ounces lemonade
Splash Clayton Distillery Raspberry Liqueur
Lemon slice

Fill glass with ice. Add ingredients, ending with the raspberry liqueur, and stir. Garnish with lemon slice.

One of the places in Clayton that captures its riverfront atmosphere is Channelside, a bar and restaurant operated by Molly and Peter Beattie. Many of its signature cocktails have nautical names, like this one.

Not a PFD
From the Channelside Restaurant, Clayton

½ ounce pomegranate liqueur
1 thick slice of fresh lemon
4 or 5 mint leaves
1 ounce Clayton Distillery Bourbon
Lemonade, to top glass

In a shaker glass, muddle pomegranate liqueur with lemon and mint leaves. Add bourbon, top off with ice and lemonade. Roll to mix contents. Pour into fresh glass. Garnish with fresh mint leaf.

7

THE TWENTIETH-CENTURY SPIRIT

STAYING ALIVE: THE STORY OF FEE BROTHERS

Legal liquor returned in 1933. But it wasn't quite the same. The business of distilling spirits wouldn't come back to Upstate New York for another seventy years or so. And as cocktail historian Ted Haigh recounts in *Vintage Spirits and Forgotten Cocktails*, the trend for much of the rest of the twentieth century was toward ever lighter drinks, from pale yellow beer and bland blended whiskey to unimaginative cocktails.

In Upstate New York, however, there were a few gleams in that otherwise dim period. It starts with a venerable Rochester company that bridged the timeline from the golden age of the late nineteenth century all the way to the cocktail resurgence of the twenty-first century: Fee Brothers.

Joe Fee, who runs the company today, sometimes thinks he'd like to go back in time and talk to his grandfather. "I want to say, 'You had a business making a product that people used by the ounce, or ounces, and then you started making a product that people use by the dash?'" Fee punctuated his question by pretending to strangle his grandfather.

Of course, Fee is kidding.

Somehow Fee Brothers of Rochester has managed to stay in business for well over one hundred years and even experience some explosive growth in the twenty-first century. It started as a liquor and wine importer and retailer and then became a winemaker. In Joe Fee's grandfather's day (around Prohibition), it began manufacturing flavored cocktail syrups (which people

Joe Fee of Fee Brothers, a maker of cocktail, bitters, syrups, mixers and such, in the company's headquarters (and museum) in Rochester. *Author's photo.*

do in fact use by the ounce) and then added the production of bitters, the cocktail ingredient that few people ever use in quantities of more than a few dashes at a time.

Now, the business is booming, thanks to a cocktail resurgence. It started, Fee said, around 1991, when the Internet was in its infancy and cocktail enthusiasts began communicating with each other on message boards and chat rooms. Then some of the most famous names in the modern world of cocktails and cocktail literature—like Dale DeGroff, Gary Regan and Ted Haigh—discovered Fee Brothers.

It turned out that this small family-run business in Rochester had spent decades producing some of the then-obscure ingredients necessary to power the cocktail craze of the early twenty-first century.

"We've always been making this stuff," said Joe Fee, who, with his sister Ellen, is part of the fourth generation to run the company. "It's just that everybody else caught up, or caught on to us."

Long gone are the days when the yearly production of some of the Fee Brothers' product lines was a mere five gallons. Growth in the second decade of the 2000s reached 300 percent per year.

Cocktailians and mixologists across the United States and around the world now know that Fee Brothers can supply their orgeat syrup (for drinks like the mai tai) or their olive brine (for dirty martinis). It's also a source for grapefruit bitters.

Your nose will tell you a lot about Fee Brothers. Walk into the production facility and retail shop in northeast Rochester and you'll be greeted by the perfume of tropical fruit, the zing of spice and sunny essence of herbs. Or a combination of all that, and more. Bottling lines hum and forklifts move pallets, just as in any manufacturing plant.

Fee Brothers is proud of its history—there's even a small museum-like space with mason jars, beakers, bar mirrors, and lab and production equipment from the past.

The story of Fee Brothers serves as a sort of timeline to the history of drinking and cocktails in America from the Civil War to the present day. The company was founded in 1863 by James Fee, the son of an Irish immigrant, and his brothers Owen, John and Joseph. (Their likenesses now adorn the company's logo.) In the latter nineteenth century, it was both a maker of wine and importer of wines and liquors.

Jug made before 1883 at Fee Brothers in Rochester. The company was founded in 1863 and continues today as a maker of bitters, cordials and other cocktail ingredients. *Author's photo.*

The start-up date led to an old jingle that Joe Fee still likes to recite: "The House of Fee / by the Genesee / since eighteen hundred and sixty-three." As with many businesses, Fee Brothers went through some trials and tribulations, including a fire in 1908 that destroyed its original building alongside the river.

It was during Prohibition—which of course put a crimp in wine production and importing—that things at Fee Brothers began to change. The company managed to cobble together some business by making altar wine for the Catholic Church and producing starter kits for home winemakers. (It was legal for people to produce a small amount of homemade wine during Prohibition.)

Fee Brothers also made a nonalcoholic malt extract beer called Bruno. According to the official company history, owner John Fee Jr. placed this warning (or hint) on the label: "Do not add yeast to this product as it is likely to ferment."

Perhaps the most significant addition to the Fee Brothers repertoire at this point was the manufacture of "flavorings." These no-alcohol cordial syrups—in flavors such as Benedictine, Chartreuse, Rum and Brandy—could be added to illegal homemade liquor, like the famed "bathtub gin," to make it more palatable. (Not that the Fees would actually advocate such an idea, of course.)

"Creme de Menthe (mint) was a very popular cordial—you could add that to the hooch and it tasted just like real Creme de Menthe," Joe Fee says.

This was the beginning of Fee Brothers status as a maker of cocktail additives.

After Prohibition, the company, now headed by a cousin also named John, went back to winemaking in addition to the new business of cordial syrups. It was in the late 1930s that John Fee developed a new product he called "Frothy Mixer." It was a lemon concentrate that added flavor to drinks like the Whiskey Sour and the Tom Collins and gave those drinks a frothy head, like beer.

That's when the company developed another catchy slogan, urging people to give up fresh lemons for their drinks: "Don't Squeeze, Use Fee's."

By the 1950s, Fee Brothers had stopped making wine and other alcohol products and moved entirely into the business of cordials, flavorings, syrups and bitters—everything from grenadine and orgeat syrups to an aromatic "Old Fashioned" bitters similar to the flagship product of the industry leader, Angostura.

Most sales were made to restaurants, bars and bar wholesalers. The head of the company at that point was Jack Fee, Joe Fee's father. In 1953, after his own father died, Jack had left a job as a chemist at Kodak, the big Rochester-based film company, to take over the family business. But Jack Fee didn't know a whole lot about making the Fee products.

"He found my grandfather's recipe book," Joe Fee said. "The problem was they were written in code. It would say, 'Take a spoon of ixmus.' Well, what's 'ixmus?' And is that a level spoon or a mounded spoon?"

Jack Fee was only able to resurrect about six of his father's thirty or so recipes, according to Joe. Tastes also changed. The company survived largely on the strength of its cordials and mixers during the 1950s and '60s. Bitters were not in style anymore. "It was horrible," Joe Fee says. "My father would make a whole year's supply of the Old Fashioned bitters in a five gallon pail."

Then, in the early 1990s came the Internet and those message boards. "Bartenders started talking to each other, relearning old skills," Fee says. "The bitters began to really take off." Above all, it was the search for orange bitters that helped bring Fee Brothers its renewed fame.

The story is recounted by drinks author and historian Ted Haigh, aka "Dr. Cocktail," in his book *Vintage Spirits and Forgotten Cocktails*. It was 1992, Haigh recalled, when he was obsessed with research on the classic drinks of a bygone age. He discovered many called for orange bitters, which he was unable to find. At that time, Angostura aromatic bitters were just about the only brand and style available.

"The most frustrating aspect was the sheer number of delicious-sounding recipes that called for orange bitters," Haigh writes. "I couldn't find those bitters anywhere. No one carried them, and I was beginning to think they were extinct."

More maddening, he came across a new book with a recipe for a drink with the evocative name Satan's Whiskers. It used orange bitters, so, Haigh reasoned, they must exist somewhere.

He eventually called Angostura, which is based in the island nation of Trinidad and Tobago, and boldly asked if they knew of a competitor who bottled orange bitters. He ended up talking to Angostura's North American executive.

"After a minimum of beating around the bush," Haigh writes, "[he] amicably said it was true, there was such a company…Fee Brothers, in Rochester, New York."

Haigh placed an order with Jack Fee and began vigorously promoting Fee Brothers in an AOL online forum and, eventually, his books. Drinks like the Arnaud's Special Cocktail, the Modernista and the Calvados Cocktail (which takes a huge ¾ of an ounce of orange bitters) probably wouldn't have made it into Haigh's book without his "discovery" of Fee Brothers.

"It turns out we were the only manufacturer of orange bitters in the world," Joe Fee says. Until then, Fee's orange bitters were sold mostly to bars and wholesalers in the Northeast.

Things have changed at Fee Brothers since then. Along with the exponential growth in the volume of bitters it produces, Fee Brothers also expanded the varieties as both professional and amateur mixologists got more creative.

"When I was a boy, we only had three bitters," Fee says, "the Old Fashioned, the orange and the mint." They started making peach bitters in the 1990s and have branched out to lemon, grapefruit and more. By 2016, there were about seventeen varieties. "Most have historic roots," Fee says. "But then Ellen and I decided, what the heck, let's try something different. It sort of became a habit."

Today, the lineup includes everything from black walnut to Aztec chocolate bitters. Syrups and cordials remain a big part of the business, as do botanical waters like rose, hibiscus and lavender and brines like olive and dill pickle. There are thirty-eight flavored syrup varieties.

A collection of Fee Brothers bitters in the tasting room at 1911 Established (Beak and Skiff Orchards) in LaFayette. *Author's photo.*

There is a lot more competition these days, Fee says. Orange bitters, for example, are now made by the large Sazerac drinks company (Regan's Orange Bitters No. 6), and even Angostura joined in.

Fee has been happy to let the cocktail cognoscenti do some of the marketing for his company. "I didn't do a lot of education [teaching people about Fee products]," he said. "I did a lot of listening, to Ted [Haigh], Dale [DeGroff] and Gary [Regan] and others. You know, I've never been a bartender myself. So it makes sense to listen to what they have to say."

Now Fee and his sister Ellen are still tinkering with new ideas. One of those is a line of shrubs—vinegar-based or preserved fruit syrups that can liven up a cocktail. They're also historic, going back to the cocktails earliest days.

The days when few people heard of Fee Brothers are over. The company still sells most of its bitters to bars and restaurants and has extended its reach across the Unites States and as far as Australia. Fee is also proud that so many of Rochester's new young bartenders now reach for the city's hometown ingredients.

The company, he notes, "hung around" long enough to be part of a rebound in tastes. "It's been an interesting ride," Fee says. "Each generation did something different with the business. We've always reinvented ourselves to fit the times."

Here's the drink that set author and cocktail historian Ted "Dr. Cocktail" Haigh on the road to "discovering" Fee Brothers orange bitters.

Satan's Whiskers

From Vintage Spirits and Forgotten Cocktails, *by Ted Haigh*

½ ounce gin
½ ounce dry vermouth
½ ounce sweet vermouth
½ ounce orange juice
2 teaspoons orange curaçao
1 teaspoon orange bitters

Shake in an iced cocktail shaker and strain into a cocktail glass. Garnish with an orange twist.

Note: A variation can be made by substituting Grand Marnier for the orange curaçao.

The following recipes come from a product "sell sheet" produced by Fee Brothers:

Brandy Melba
From Fee Brothers

2 dashes Fee's Orange Bitters
¼ ounce Fee's Peach Cordial Syrup
¼ ounce Fee's Raspberry Cordial Syrup
½ ounce Fee's Whiskey Sour Mix
1 ½ ounces brandy

Shake with ice and strain into a cocktail glass. Garnish with a peach slice

"Classic" Martini
From Fee Brothers

2 to 3 dashes Fee's Orange Bitters
2 ounces gin
¾ ounce dry vermouth

Stir with ice, strain into a martini glass. Garnish with an olive.

Note: "Orange bitters remained an ingredient in Dry Martinis right through to the 1930s," author Gary Regan writes in his 2003 book, *The Joy of Mixology*. It was the late 1940s when the Dry Martini became just gin and vermouth (and not much vermouth at that).

FICTION, FACT AND THE FLAMING RUM PUNCH

The air is cold. The snow is falling. An iron bridge over an icy river is silhouetted against the snow. Is that a man preparing to jump in the river? Is that a would-be angel, ready to save him?

You might think it's 1946 and you're in Bedford Falls, setting of the classic Christmas film *It's a Wonderful Life*. Or you could be in Seneca Falls, the real-life Upstate New York town that bills itself, each December, as the "real Bedford Falls."

View from the "George Bailey Bridge" in Seneca Falls, which styles itself "Bedford Falls" each holiday season in tribute to the movie *It's a Wonderful Life. Author's photo.*

As we've seen, fact and fiction often intersect in the story of cocktails. This story starts as pure fiction, but it has taken on a dose of reality in recent years.

You remember the movie, released in 1946: George Bailey (played by Jimmy Stewart) is feeling despondent on Christmas Eve and ends up on the bridge. The angel, Clarence, saves him by showing what the world, or at least his hometown of Bedford Falls, would be like if he had never been born.

Seneca Falls looks the part. The main street, Fall Street, is lined with shops housed in mid-nineteenth and early twentieth-century buildings. That iron bridge could have been lifted straight off the movie set. (It's now called George Bailey Bridge.)

Seneca Falls points to several indicators that it could be the inspiration for Bedford Falls, including one character's reference to Elmira being just an hour away and other mentions of Rochester and Buffalo being nearby. Also, some townspeople believe legendary director Frank Capra visited Seneca Falls before making the film.

Each December, Seneca Falls hosts a weekend-long celebration, complete with visits by surviving actors from the film and local folks dressed up as Uncle Billy, Ma Bailey, Mr. Potter and other characters. There's a parade, and shops offer specials.

On Fall Street, a historic hotel drapes a sign out front, billing itself as "Martini's," the bar frequented by George Bailey in the film. It's really the Gould Hotel and its restaurant, which a few years ago briefly renamed itself the Clarence. At the Gould, the film runs without sound in a continuous loop, projected on the wall behind the front desk.

So what does all this have to do with cocktails?

Consider this scene, which takes place during the sequence in which George has "never been born." The setting is Martini's (renamed after the new owner, Nick, at this point in the film):

> *George: Oh, hello, Nick. Hey, where's Martini?*
> *Nick: You want a martini?*
> *George: No, no, Martini. Your boss. Where is he?*
> *Nick: Look, I'm the boss. You want a drink or don't you?*
> *George: Okay…all right. Double bourbon, quick, huh?*
> *Nick: Okay.* [to Clarence] *What's yours?*
> *Clarence: I was just thinking….It's been so long since I…*
> *Nick: Look, mister, I'm standing here waiting for you to make up your mind.*
> *Clarence: That's a good man. I was just thinking of a flaming rum punch. No, it's not cold enough for that. Not nearly cold enough….Wait a minute…wait a minute….Mulled wine, heavy on the cinnamon and light on the cloves. Off with you, me lad, and be lively!*
> *Nick: Hey, look mister, we serve hard drinks in here for men who want to get drunk fast. And we don't need any characters around to give the joint atmosphere. Is that clear? Or do I have to slip you my left for a convincer?*
> *Clarence:* [to George] *What's he talking about?*
> *George: Nick—Nick, just give him the same as mine. He's okay.*
> *Nick: Okay.*
> *George: What's the matter with him? I never saw Nick act like that before.*
> *Clarence: You'll see a lot of strange things from now on.*

The flaming rum punch was a favorite in the eighteen and early nineteenth centuries, mentioned in the writings of Charles Dickens, among others. By the 1940s, when *It's A Wonderful Life* takes place, the flaming rum punch, like many other styles of punch, had gone out of style.

But, like many classic drinks, it's made a comeback. And while in olden days it was often mixed in big batches and served in a punch bowl, today's punches are often single drinks.

Just before Christmas 2009, chef Ed Moro, then the food and beverage director at the Hotel Clarence in Seneca Falls, came up with a modern version of the rum punch for a story that appeared in the *Syracuse Post-Standard* and syracuse.com. His was an individual drink. More recently, the team at the Gould (formerly the Clarence) re-created Moro's version. Chrissy Kennedy, food and beverage manager for Hospitality Concepts, and owner Ben Eberhardt concocted this version at the Gould on Bedford Falls weekend in 2016.

Flaming Rum Punch
Adapted from Ed Moro and the Gould Hotel

Orange wedge, for rimming glass
Sugar, for rimming glass
1 ½ ounces white rum
Splash cherry brandy
Large splash fresh orange juice
Large splash pineapple juice (equal to orange juice)
Splash grenadine
1 ounce 151-proof rum

Using a stemmed glass, sugar the rim of the glass with juice from a slice of orange. In a separate mixing glass, add ice, white rum, cherry brandy, orange juice and pineapple juice. Strain into martini glass (or wine glass). Add grenadine, as it will settle to the bottom and give a layered look. Float the 151 rum on the top. Light the 151 rum and let burn for a few seconds until the sugar is caramelized and then blow out the flame.

Note: In his original version, Ed Moro sugared the rim of the glass, added the 151-proof rum and flamed it to caramelize the sugar. Then he mixed and strained the other ingredients into the glass. Either way, it's important to use a tempered (heat-resistant) glass.

Borscht Belt: Bungalows and Highballs

In mid-twentieth-century America, drinking had become fairly standardized. Yet there was one section of Upstate New York where, even if the martinis were the same as everywhere else, the ambience was all its own. It was the so-called "Borscht Belt," the string of hotels, "bungalow colonies" and resorts in New York's Catskill Mountain region that catered primarily to Jewish customers.

"At any given time in the 1950s and 1960s, there were about 500 of those colonies and 550 hotels operating," writes Phil Brown in an essay called "The Legacy of the Jewish Catskills." "An estimated one million people vacationed there in that period."

"A sense of community pervaded the Catskills," writes Brown, whose parents once owned a small Catskills hotel and who worked there and elsewhere when he was young. He's now a professor of sociology at Brown University and a founder of the Catskills Institute. "Guests returned year after year, and often from generation to generation....Guests developed a loyalty to the hotel and its owners, based on family, friendship and on participating in a miniature society where relationships were amplified by the proximity."

And of course, there was the legendary entertainment. Noted comics and entertainers from Milton Berle to Jerry Seinfeld played in the Catskill resorts. And there were bars. But the drinks at the bars seemed to fit squarely within the tastes of midcentury America: martinis, Manhattans and plenty of highballs—the gin and tonic, for example. An old bar menu for Kutsher's Hotel near Monticello also lists some classic twentieth-century cocktails, like the Between the Sheets and the Zombie.

"Over the course of the years we had an active bar and service bar with talented bartenders who could mix many cocktails," Mark Kutsher wrote in an e-mail to the author. He's a member of the family that owned Kutsher's, which began fading in the 1990s and finally closed for good in 2013. "I feel badly reporting that our menus did not have any customized Catskill or Kutsher's cocktails. If I were still operating today with the heated up cocktail scene, I can assure you we would have some great cocktails."

It might indeed be different if the resorts were around today, but all the grand hotels are gone, leaving a few bungalow colonies and the promise of future development. One place where there has been development is the small village of Sharon Springs, just a little north of the Catskill region. It was once home to a number of hotels that were patronized primarily by Hasidic Jews. It's here you'll find the American Hotel, reopened and operated since 2001 by Garth Roberts and Doug Plummer. It was built in the 1840s and was once known as the Kosher American Hotel. Today,

Right: A late twentieth-century drinks menu from the Palestra at Kutsher's Country Club, a resort in the Catskills town of Monticello. *Courtesy of Mark Kutsher.*

Below: A late twentieth-century drinks list from the Palestra at Kutsher's Country Club, a resort in the Catskills town of Monticello. *Courtesy of Mark Kutsher.*

The Palestra - - - - Sportsmen's Loung

(Fun starts in the a.

| Flamingo | .75 | Flamingo with Rum or Gin | 1.25 |
| Champagne Cocktail | 1.25 | Atom Bomb | 1.50 |

Alexander	1.00	Manhattan	.75
Alexander Brandy	1.00	Martini	.75
Bacardi	.75	Gibson	.75
Daiquiri	.75	Old Fashioned	.75
Screw Driver	.85	Orange Blossom	.75
Jack Rose	.75	Pink Lady	1.00
Side Car	.85	Stinger	.85
Whiskey Sour	.75	Cherry Herring Mist	1.00
Grasshopper	1.00	Between the Sheets	.85

3e Palestra (Energy Reviver) for two $3.00

LONG DRINKS		CORDIALS	
Gin and Tonic	.75	Creme de Cocoa	.65
		Kijafa Cherry	.65
Rum and Coke	.65	Cherry Herring	.90
Cuba Libre	.75	Apricot	.75
		Blackberry	.75
Singapore Sling	.85	Creme de Menthe	.75
		Cointreau	.75
Planters Punch	1.00	Drambuie	.90
Zombie	1.50	B. & B.	1.00

WINES			
			Bot.
B & G Sauterne	.75	6.00	
Burgundy	.75	6.00	

PORT		SHERRY	
Imp.	.75	Imp.	
Dom.	.60	Dom.	

CHAMPAGNES			
Domestic	$7.50 per Bot.		
Imported	12.00 per Bot.		

SCOTCHES		RYE WHISKIES	
Ballantine	.75	Canadian Club	
Black & White	.75	Seagram's VO	
Cutty Sark	.75	Seagram's 7 Crown	
J. B.	.75	Imperial	
Dewar's White Label	.75	Schenley	
Haig & Haig 5	.75	Calverts	
Haig & Haig Pinch	.85	Four Roses	
Johnny Walker Red	.75	Carstairs	
Johnny Walker Black	.85	Vodka Smirnoff (100 proof)	
King's Ransom	.85	BONDED BOURBON	
Chivas Regal	1.00	I. W. Harper	
Ambassador, 10 yr.	.85	Old Grandad	
Ambassador, 25 yr.	1.25	Old Forrester	
		Old Taylor	

BOTTLED BEER		BRANDY	
Budweiser	.50	Domestic	
Reingold	.50	Remy Martin	
Imp. Ale	.65	Remy Martin VSOP	
Heinekens	.75	Hennessy	
All Soft Drinks	.25	Courvoisier	

119

The American Hotel in Sharon Springs. *Author's photo.*

The American Hotel Martini, made with Cooperstown Distillery's Glimmerglass Vodka at the American Hotel in Sharon Springs. *Author's photo.*

it is directly across the street from the Beekman 1802 Mercantile store, made famous in TV's *The Fabulous Beekman Boys*.

The town is noted for its mineral water springs, which were touted for their health benefits as far back as colonial days. One spring, in Chalybeate Park, was said by the Native Americans to be good for the eyes. "We were always a little more health-minded here than the Catskills," Plummer said, noting the local spring's slogan: "Bathe in it. Drink It. Inhale it."

The bar at the American Hotel today is a fine place to stop in for drinks that take note of local history and lore. On our visit, bartender George VanGarderen mixed up a few, including this make-ahead cocktail.

Mapple Jack Moonrise
From the American Hotel, Sharon Springs

1 bottle of Schoharie Mapple Jack (see note)
¼ cup vanilla bean paste (or real beans)
4 to 6 cinnamon sticks
4 Granny Smith apples, cut up
2 Bosch pears, cut up
4 to 6 cinnamon sticks

Mix all ingredients and marinate in refrigerator for two weeks. Strain and serve neat or on the rocks.

Note: Schoharie Mapple Jack is an apple brandy flavored with maple syrup, made by KyMar Farm Winery and Distillery in Schoharie County in the northern Catskills. Plummer suggests using the fruit left over from the marinade over ice cream. The Moonrise, he says, "is a great snuggle drink."

Harvey Wallbanger:
The Cocktail Mascot of the 1970s

The 1970s may not have been the most classic, or classy, era in cocktails. But it did feature some amazing, and amazingly named, mixed drinks. And one of those had a remarkable connection to Upstate New York.

The drink is the Harvey Wallbanger. You may remember it: a mix of vodka, orange juice and a splash of the Italian liqueur Galliano. If you remember it, you can thank William J. "Bill" Young, an advertising man with a studio in Lima, New York, south of Rochester.

It was Young who, in late 1969, concocted the campaign that brought the Harvey Wallbanger to the attention of all those future disco-loving, platform shoe–wearing, Me Generation drinkers. His Lima studio, called Young Ideas, had been hired by McKesson Imports Company, which brought Galliano to the United States from Italy and was looking for a way to promote it.

Young didn't invent the drink—and there's some dispute over who did. He did come up with ads that featured a cartoon character named, you guessed it, Harvey Wallbanger. The character's

William J. "Bill" Young, the Lima, New York advertising man who came up with the campaign for the Harvey Wallbanger cocktail in the 1970s. *Courtesy of Will Young.*

catchphrase was "Harvey Wallbanger's the name and I can be made!"

He wasn't exactly "the most interesting man in the world" (to cite an early twenty-first-century campaign for Dos Equis beer), but he might have been a sort of '70s equivalent. After Young's death in October 2016, David Andreatta of the *Rochester Democrat & Chronicle* wrote of the character: "The mascot…was a bleary-eyed, big-footed dude who surfed, skydived, lifeguarded and even ran for president, always wearing a vacant expression of distress. Picture an overweight, hungover Linus Van Pelt fretting over his security blanket and you have Harvey Wallbanger in all situations."

Yet the campaign was a huge success.

A history of the drink written by Robert Simonson in a 2012 issue of *Saveur* magazine reports Young's "cartoon figure hit the U.S. like a lava flow in late 1969." Simonson cited a 1969 report in the *San Antonio Light*, which said the Harvey Wallbanger campaign included "pop art posters, bumper stickers, buttons, crew shirts, mugs and the whole bit."

"Soon, reports were cropping up of bowls of Wallbangers being consumed at Hamptons parties and on Amtrak trains," Simonson writes.

"By 1976, Holland House was putting out a Wallbanger dry mix and pre-blended bottles of the cocktail were sold. Riding this wave, Galliano became the number one most imported liqueur during the Me Decade, exporting 500,000 cases a year to the U.S."

The drink itself may have been invented in California in the 1950s, perhaps by a noted mixologist named Donato "Duke" Antone, also known for coming up with a drink called the Freddie Fudpucker, and possibly others like the White Russian, the Rusty Nail and the Kamikaze. Simonson and other writers dispute many of these claims, and the real origins remain unknown.

There's no doubt the Harvey Wallbanger was a '70s phenomenon. "With Young's Harvey to blaze the way," cocktail historian David Wondrich says in Simonson's *Saveur* piece, "Antone's simple—even dopey—drink would go on to be the first drink created by a consultant to actually take the nation by storm."

Simonson himself was not much of a fan.

"The Harvey Wallbanger has one of the most memorable names in cocktail history—and one of the worst reputations," is how he begins his *Saveur* piece, titled "Searching for Harvey Wallbanger." "A mix of vodka, orange juice and Galliano," Simonson writes. "it was one of the preeminent drinks of the 1970s, a decade recognized by drink historians as the Death Valley of cocktail eras: a time of sloppy, foolish drinks made with sour mix and other risible shortcuts to flavor, christened with silly monikers like Mudslide and Freddie Fudpucker."

As for Young, his son, Will, told the *Democrat & Chronicle*'s Andreatta that his father built a successful ad career, given a large boost by Harvey. Bill Young apparently got a percentage of each case of Galliano imported to the United States.

"I don't remember much, but I remember when all of a sudden my dad went from driving a Volkswagen to a BMW," Will Young told Andreatta. "Our whole world changed with the Harvey Wallbanger."

The Galliano company (now part of Lucas Bols in the Netherlands) remembered its debt to Bill Young when he passed away in Canandaigua, New York, in 2016. "They sent a bunch of Galliano so we could make Harvey Wallbangers at his memorial service," Will Young said.

The official Galliano company recipe, often appearing on Young's posters, was six parts orange juice, three parts vodka, lots of ice and a splash of Galliano. Here's one that accompanied Simonson's *Saveur* article:

Harvey Wallbanger

From Saveur.com

1 ounce vodka
4 ounces orange juice
½ ounce Galliano liqueur

Pour vodka and orange juice into an ice-filled collins glass. Stir. Float Galliano on top by pouring gently over the back of a spoon.

8
RESURGENCE AND REVIVAL

THE DRINKS RENAISSANCE BEGINS

From the days when classic and creative cocktails were all but forgotten and the spirits that propelled them were mass-produced and often watered down, we've come full circle. The twenty-first century has brought a revival, not only in the art of well-crafted mixed drinks but also in the small-batch distillers and other producers who prize quality and take pride in using locally made and grown ingredients.

Joe Fee, of Rochester's mixer and bitter maker Fee Brothers, credits the Internet as a spark. Bartenders and others interested in good drinks and their ingredients began talking to one another in forums and other online venues. They shared recipes and helped one another find ingredients. Then came the cocktail-oriented books and magazine articles by authors cited throughout this book, such as William Grimes, Ted Haigh, Gary Regan and David Wondrich. Demand for such items as small-batch bourbon and orange bitters soared.

"We hung around long enough until everybody found us," said Fee, whose company, founded in 1863, spans more than half the time frame covered in this book.

Of course, there were other factors, including the farm-to-table movement and, in New York at least, a relaxing of some of the strict alcohol regulations that had accompanied the repeal of Prohibition. Whatever the reasons, Upstate New York finds itself in a spirits and cocktail renaissance.

Firing Up Upstate New York's Stills at Last

Doug and Suzie Knapp were already successful winemakers when they purchased an alembic still—modeled on the earliest type of distilling apparatus—in 1994. They used it, starting in 1995, to make brandy from wine at their Knapp Winery, on Cayuga Lake in the Finger Lakes. Knapp produced the first commercial distilled spirit in New York since Prohibition. Another Finger Lakes winery, Swedish Hill, soon followed suit.

But that was just a prelude. A decade later, in 2005, Ralph Erenzo and his partner Brian Lee opened New York State's first post-Prohibition standalone distillery (and maker of whiskey).

"Now look what we've created," said Erenzo, of Tuthilltown Spirits and Hudson Whiskey in Gardiner, which includes a stillhouse, tasting room and restaurant. (The whole operation was sold to the Scottish distiller William Grant & Sons, in 2017.) "We were once the only distillery in New York. Now there's a whole distilling industry."

By 2017, New York State had issued about 175 distilling licenses, most of them in Upstate New York. Many were issued to what are known as farm distillers, those who pledge to use New York–grown and produced ingredients in return for breaks on fees and easing of regulations.

Ralph Erenzo, co-founder of Tuthilltown Spirits/Hudson Whiskeys in Gardiner, the first standalone distillery in New York State since Prohibition. *Author's photo.*

The craft of distilling has returned to Upstate New York.

Distilleries now can be found everywhere Upstate—in the Hudson Valley and along the St. Lawrence River, in the Adirondacks and the Finger Lakes, in Albany, Utica, Rochester and Buffalo. They're following the path shared by New York's booming wine, craft beer and hard cider businesses.

It took a little longer for the hard spirits industry to get restarted after Prohibition. Wineries and breweries in New York reopened in 1933, but not distilleries. The surge in New York alcohol production we see today began with the state's approval of the Farm Winery Act of 1976. It allowed small wine producers to sell their products directly to consumers—out of their own tasting rooms and without the need to go through wholesalers—in return for using New York grapes. The state's winery boom began then, leading to more than four hundred wineries by 2017.

The 1976 winery law was the state's first major effort to reform or abolish some of the restrictive alcohol laws put in place after Prohibition and untangle the bureaucratic web that made the liquor business difficult to enter.

Craft breweries followed. A few started up in the 1980s, growing, first erratically and then steadily, to about one hundred by 2012. At that point, the administration of Governor Andrew Cuomo, taking a cue from the farm winery act, worked with the state brewers' association to enact a similar farm brewery bill that offered benefits for using New York ingredients. From 2012 to 2017, the number of breweries surged to more than three hundred.

Distilling came along more slowly. Tuthilltown had got the ball rolling, and Erenzo helped get a farm distillery bill passed in 2007—even earlier than the brewery version. "It was brilliant," Erenzo said. "Here was law that turned your distillery into a farm, and as a farm you didn't need to go through the three-tiered system [manufacturer to wholesaler to retailer]. We could sell our own stuff to our own customers and keep the money."

A few more craft or farm distilleries started cropping up around 2009. Then, the farm distillery law was amended to offer even more benefits in 2014—notably the ability to sell other New York alcoholic beverages and even cocktails in the tasting room. That's when craft distillers finally began to show up in bigger numbers.

Of course, all this coincided with the buy local, farm-to-table (or field-to-glass) movement that has become a big part of the national foodscape. That was important, because craft spirits, even more than craft beer or wine, finds itself in a specialty or niche segment of the market.

"Craft spirits are a little more expensive," said Jason Barrett, owner of Black Button Distilling in Rochester, which hit the market in 2014. "So you have to have a little money and an interest in where your food comes from. People have to make that transition away from quantity over quality—they need to think about what they're getting and where they get it from."

In New York, the state continued to ease rules for all beverage manufacturers—notably allowing the sales of alcoholic beverages, including cocktails, in tasting rooms. Governor Cuomo began hosting craft beverage "summits" to find out what more the state can do to promote the industry.

Cornell University in Ithaca, which had been using its resources and research to aid wineries since the late 1800s, began turning more of its attention to brewing, hard cider and distilling. Cornell, which has a state-supported agriculture program, helps with everything from the types of grain to plant to best practices in the stillhouse.

"Because of the success we've had with wineries, and breweries, and hard cider, we have the infrastructure in New York State to help the distilleries," said Chris Gerling, an extension associate at the New York State Agricultural Experiment Station in Geneva in the Finger Lakes. "I think we can help the distillers figure out how to differentiate themselves, how to establish an identity."

Jason Barrett, president and founder of Black Button Distilling in Rochester. *Author's photo.*

Modern Distilleries: Five to Watch

Today's Upstate New York distilleries come in all sizes. They make all sorts of spirits, and use just about every conceivable base ingredient, from apples, grapes and honey to corn, wheat and rye. We've introduced some of them in previous chapters. Here's a look at some of the other notable Upstate New York distilleries (and some of their signature cocktails).

Tuthilltown Spirits/Hudson Whiskey, Gardiner

Ralph Erenzo and Brian Lee are universally acknowledged as the pioneers of modern New York craft distilling. They opened their distillery in Gardiner, near New Paltz, in 2005. The project was initially intended to be a "climber's ranch," where those tackling the nearby Shawangunk Mountains could stay during their expeditions. Neighbors opposed the plan. "The neighbors threw up every obstacle to the ranch," Erenzo says, "but they didn't know me very well. I'm a terrier."

With his first dream dashed, Erenzo figured out what else he might do with the thirty-six-acre property, which was zoned for farming and could be used for a winery. He didn't want to farm, and he didn't want to start a winery, which were becoming plentiful at that point.

Instead, he turned to distilling.

"Really the reason was because it was something nobody else was doing," he said. "And it wasn't rocket science. You could do it with determination and a reasonable amount of education." Meanwhile, Erenzo also found a loophole in the tangle of state alcohol laws that allowed him to get into small-batch distilling at a lower license fee ($1,500 instead of $65,000). "I thought, 'I wouldn't risk $65,000 but I might risk $1,500.'"

He also knew he wanted to make whiskey, not just fruit brandies like the wineries were doing or just clear spirits like vodka or gin. He and Lee hit the jackpot with Hudson Baby Bourbon, made from 100 percent corn. Today, the distillery makes six whiskeys, two vodkas and a gin, plus a cassis, some flavored liqueurs and cocktails bitters.

Tuthilltown's success attracted the interest of some buyers. It started in 2010, when Erenzo and Lee sold their whiskey brands, made under the name Hudson, to William Grant & Sons, a family-owned maker of scotch. Then, in April 2017, Grant bought the whole business, keeping Erenzo on as a consultant.

The Basil & Bourbon cocktail from the Tuthill House restaurant at the Tuthilltown Spirits distillery. *Author's photo.*

Basil & Bourbon
From Tuthill House at the Mill, Gardiner

1 ½ ounces Hudson Baby Bourbon
Several leaves of basil
¾ ounce Demarara sugar
¾ ounce fresh lime juice

Combine all ingredients in a shaker and shake for a few seconds. Strain contents into a small coupe. To garnish, take a piece of basil, gently smack it to release the oils and place it on the top of the drink

1911 Established/Beak & Skiff Apple Orchards, LaFayette

When life gives you apples, what do you make of it? At Beak & Skiff Apple Orchards in LaFayette, just south of Syracuse, they have lots of ideas. Beak & Skiff started in 1911 and sold apples wholesale for decades, before starting a you-pick retail operation in 1975 and producing its own fresh apple cider in 1979. By the start of the twenty-first century, Steve Morse, a manager at the growing family-owned business, saw the need to diversify—in part, to compensate for bad years in the orchard. Morse knew he could press the juice out of even ugly weather-damaged apples and make alcoholic spirits from it.

Hard cider started in 2001 and vodka, distilled from hard cider, in 2009. (Morse had to battle the impression from some drinkers that the vodka would actually taste like apples.) That was followed in the next few years by apple-based gin and a vanilla chai vodka. In 2017, the company started down the road to making its first whiskey. That will be aged in oak a full three years, meaning it can't be sold until 2020. It's the first 1911 spirit not made from apples—it's a four-grain whiskey (corn, wheat, rye and barley). "You have to stay on top of, or ahead of the market, and at the same time try make something different," said Ed Brennan, who by 2017 had become general manager at Beak & Skiff.

In less than ten years, 1911 Established had become one of the Upstate's best-known distillers, sold throughout New York. It also features a 1911 Tasting Room and Café, along with the gift shop and apple-picking visitors' center at its main campus in LaFayette.

Hot Chai-der
From 1911 Established

4 ounces Beak & Skiff fresh sweet apple cider
1½ ounces 1911 Vanilla Chai Vodka
1 apple slice
1 cinnamon stick

Heat the fresh cider and pour into a mug. Add vodka and garnish with apple slice and cinnamon stick.

Orchard Breeze
From 1911 Established

1½ ounces 1911 vodka
4 ounces Beak & Skiff fresh sweet apple cider
Splash of cranberry juice (about ½ ounce)
1 lime wedge

Fill a 12-ounce cup with ice and add the vodka, apple cider and cranberry juice. Garnish with lime wedge.

Finger Lakes Distilling Company, Burdett

Brian McKenzie built his distillery in the heart of what is known as the "Banana Belt" of the Finger Lakes, the stretch along Route 414 on the southeast shore of Seneca Lake that boasts one of the densest concentrations of wineries in the region. Finger Lakes Distilling soon became a destination of its own.

Finger Lakes produces whiskey, gin, vodka, brandy and grappa and liqueurs. It makes use of almost every kind of base ingredient the region can produce: apples, berries, grapes, honey, maple, barley, wheat and corn. Its aged McKenzie Bourbon and McKenzie Rye are "neck and neck" as bestsellers, Brian McKenzie says, in keeping with the resurgence of brown spirits across the state. Those two spirits, along with McKenzie Pure Pot Still Whiskey and its gin are sold through distributors across New York and as far away as California.

It's also become one of the state's biggest and best known distilleries, producing about four barrels a day, five days a week. About half is sold through distributors and half directly out of the tasting room. "Tourism is important to our business," said McKenzie, "We're in a great location to pick up tourists. People visiting the area want to buy and taste local products."

At the tasting room, the flavored liqueurs are popular, and so is grappa, an Italian-style brandy. It's distilled from grape pomace (seeds, skins and stalks discarded after the winemaking process). It is popular with wine-country visitors (and made by several of the wineries themselves).

When it opened in 2009, Finger Lakes Distilling had just the second farm distillery license in the state. Now it has more than one hundred competitors. McKenzie, who has also served as president of the New York State Distillers Guild, has no problem with that.

"There is certainly more noise in the market," he said. "But the more distilleries there are, the more people pay attention to what we're all doing. That's a good thing."

White Pike Mojito
From Finger Lakes Distilling

10 fresh mint leaves
2 teaspoons superfine sugar
1 ounce fresh lime juice
2 ounces Finger Lakes White Pike Whiskey
Club soda

In a rocks glass, muddle together mint leaves and sugar. Add lime juice and stir until sugar is dissolved. Add ice, followed by White Pike Whiskey and stir again. Top with club soda to taste.

Finger Lakes R&R (Rye & Rhubarb)
From Finger Lakes Distilling

2½ ounces McKenzie Rye Whiskey
2 ounces rhubarb simple syrup
½ ounce fresh lemon juice
1 to 2 dashes rhubarb bitters

Shake all ingredients and strain into a rocks glass over ice. Garnish with a rhubarb stalk and a lemon twist.

Black Button Distilling Company, Rochester

"Live Large in Small Batches" is the motto of Rochester's Black Button Distilling Company. Spend time with founder Jason Barrett, and it does seem he's living large. He's enthusiastic about his business. And why not? His family ran a button business, which he worked in when he was younger. Now, he makes whiskey. That's got to be more fun than buttons.

Barrett's drive inspires what he does. He likes wheated bourbon, so he makes a Four Grain Bourbon with a relatively high amount of wheat. He wanted a gin that stands out, so his is a Citrus Forward Gin.

Black Button started production in 2013 and sold its first products in 2014. It's located just down the street from the Rochester Public Market, next to and in a building owned by Rohrbach Brewing Company, the city's oldest craft brewer. Its products cover a broad range from Apple Pie Moonshine to Bespoke Bourbon Cream.

Barrett thinks whiskey is the future for craft distilleries, especially his own. "Gin drinkers tend to be brand loyal," he said. "Bourbon drinkers like to like a selection, picking something depending on what mood they're in. Besides, my passion is bourbon, so why don't I stick to what I like?"

585 Cocktail
From Black Button Distilling

½ ounce Black Button Citrus Forward Gin
1 ½ ounce Black Button Bourbon Cream
2 ounces cold brew coffee
2 dashes Fee Brothers Orange Bitters
2 dashes Fee Brothers Chocolate Bitters

Add all ingredients to an ice-filled rocks glass and stir.

Lockhouse Distillery, Buffalo

The first distillery in the city of Buffalo since Prohibition occupies a pretty sweet spot in the city's Cobblestone District, in the redeveloped Canalside area where the old Erie Canal once emptied into Lake Erie. It's also near the arena where the Buffalo Sabres play hockey. Lockhouse started making spirits in 2012 and moved to this location in 2015. It has a stillhouse, tasting room and bar.

Lockhouse products include grape-based vodka and both an unaged and slightly aged "barreled" gin, plus Revolution Coffee Liqueur, made with espresso. Perhaps its most unusual spirit is Ibisco Bitter, made with hibiscus flower, vanilla bean, yohimbe bark, chamomile flower, gentian root and fresh grapefruit peels. It's earthy, floral, bitter and sweet. It's Lockhouse's version of an Italian bitter aperitif, similar to Campari or Aperol. It's one way to make an Upstate New York–based Negroni.

By 2018, Lockhouse plans to produce a whiskey, to be aged not less than two years, in fifty-five-gallon barrels. (Many new distilleries speed up the process for their first whiskeys by using smaller barrels—like five to fifteen gallons—and aging for only six months or a year.) "We're going to do it right," says Lockhouse operations manager Cory Muscato.

Muscato, who joined Lockhouse after it opened and is now a partner along with Niko Georgiadis, Chad Vosseller, Thomas Jablonski and Jon Mirro, is happy to be part of what has been a remarkable economic turnaround in Buffalo in recent years.

"All the brewers and distillers and cocktail bars—it's all good," he said. "It's more people banging the same drum, but louder."

What She's Having
From Lockhouse Distillery, Buffalo

1 ½ ounces Lockhouse Ibisco Bitter Liqueur
½ ounce lemon juice
1 ounce apple walnut syrup (see note)
Prosecco
Dehydrated apple and cinnamon, for garnish

Mix Ibisco, lemon juice and syrup in an ice-filled cocktail shaker. Shake for about 20 seconds and then pour into a sparkling wine flute. Top with Prosecco, sprinkle with grated cinnamon and garnish with dehydrated apple.

Note: To make apple walnut syrup, bring 1 quart of water to a boil with ¼ cup of walnuts and 3 apples (cut-up and skin-on). Once it boils, strain out the solids and put apple water back into pot; add 1 quart sugar and stir to dissolve. Let cool, then bottle.

THE COCKTAIL REVIVAL: ROCHESTER

Of all the cities in Upstate New York, none seems to have embraced the new culture of the cocktail more than Rochester. You can see it in the fact that by 2017, the city had the fastest-growing chapter of the United States Bartenders' Guild in the country.

You can also see it at the annual Rochester Cocktail Revival, held throughout the city each year in early May. It's part pub crawl and part series of educational seminars. Mostly, it's a celebration of the renewed interest in well-crafted mixed drinks in Rochester. The revival is the brainchild of Chuck Cerankosky, who has had a hand in the rebirth of the city's cocktail culture through his association with two of its better bars: Good Luck and Cure.

Cerankosky began his career in the coffee business but quickly saw the potential in the craft cocktail scene. "With coffee, I had an interest in the origins and how it's made," Cerankosky said. He applied that to cocktails, back when a lot of people still thought "cocktail" and "martini" were synonymous. There were lots of blended, fruity drinks.

"I thought there's got to be a better way to do this," he said. "And in some ways, it turned out to be easier than I expected. It's actually harder to make a latte than a Negroni."

Although Upstate New York is generally a few years behind places like New York City in many fads and trends, Rochester embraced the return of the well-crafted cocktail. "There's some magic to being in a well-run bar that takes its time to purvey not only an art form where mixologists create cocktails on the spot, but to be able to showcase flavors that make patrons feel good," Cerankosky said in a 2015 interview with *Edible Finger Lakes* magazine. "This balance depends on an intense skill level—one that Rochester's cocktail scene is pulling off on par with the larger markets."

The Rochester Cocktail Revival started in 2014 and has attracted thousands of thirsty visitors to what Katrina Tulloch, writing for NYup.com in 2016, called its "boozy banquets and spirited soirees." The weeklong event includes tastings and demonstrations and seminars that have been led by such cocktail luminaries as Dale DeGroff, Robert Simonson and Gary Regan. In 2016, one highlight was a demonstration on making the perfect James Bond (Vesper) Martini.

In addition to Cerankosky's own bars, participants have included some of the other places in town noted for good drinks: Cheshire, the Revelry, Ox & Stone, the Daily Refresher, Roux, the Cub Room, Nosh and more. Producers like Fee Brothers—the bitters, cordial and syrup maker—and Black Button Distilling are also involved.

Using those local companies' products in his bars, and showcasing them at the revival, has been a plus, Cerankosky said. "It's great to be able to use those spirits in our bar program.…At first, we used them to be polite. Now, we use them because they're good."

Here is a drink created by cocktail writer Robert Hess in tribute to the city, with a nod to Professor Jerry Thomas.

Rochester Cocktail
From Robert Hess (drinkboy.com)

2 ounces rye whiskey
1 ounce Dubonnet
½ ounce Licor 43 (a Spanish liqueur)
¼ ounce absinthe
2 dashes Angostura bitters (note)

Add all the spirits with a couple dashes of bitters into a cocktail shaker with ice. Shake up and strain into a cocktail glass.

Note: To make this more authentically "Rochester," try substituting Fee Brothers Old Fashion Aromatic Bitters, similar in style to Angostura.

EXCELSIOR: ALL NEW YORK, ALL THE TIME

If there is one place where the union of New York spirits and cocktails reaches its pinnacle, it might be the Excelsior Pub in downtown Albany, just a few blocks from the state capitol. Jason "Jay" Bowers operates the pub on one guiding principle: all the beer, wine and spirits are made in New York State. That means most come from Upstate.

"If you give New Yorkers a chance to have some state pride, they'll love it," Bowers said. "They'll just grab it. Every time."

He shares that spirit when it comes to sales representatives who come into his pub bearing New York products. He's been known to buy them at first sight. "If it's made in New York, I'm an easy mark," he said.

Owner Jason "Jay" Bowers in the Excelsior Pub in Albany. The pub exclusively serves New York State beer, wine and spirits. *Author's photo.*

If you think it would be hard to stock a full-service bar with only New York beers, wine and spirits, Bowers is here to disagree. He even makes that New Orleans classic, the Sazerac, with an Upstate New York–based absinthe, made by the Delaware Phoenix Distillery in the Catskills town of Walton. The pub's food menu also pays tribute to New York cuisine, from Buffalo's beef on weck sandwich to Rochester's "garbage plate" and Binghamton's spiedies.

"Having things from New York that no one else has—that's my bread and butter," he said.

Capital Apple
From the Excelsior Pub, Albany

2 ounces 1911 Vodka
Splash of sweet cider
½ ounce cinnamon simple syrup
Piece of cooked apple for garnish

Put vodka, cider and simple syrup into ice-filled shaker. Shake and strain into martini glass. Garnish with pieces of apple skewered on toothpick.

Excelsior Sazerac
From the Excelsior Pub, Albany

Delaware Phoenix Absinthe
3 dashes Peychauds bitters
Sugar, to taste
Water
2 ounces Hudson Manhattan Rye (Tuthilltown)
Lemon twist

Swirl absinthe in a small tumbler or rocks glass and discard. Muddle bitters, sugar and water in bottom of mixing glass. Add ice and rye, then stir and strain into absinthe-rinsed glass. Garnish with lemon twist.

The Cocktail Test Kitchen

In the modern, fast-paced world, it's not enough to create a cocktail list and leave it at that. You have to change it up.

Like some drinks, the list needs to be freshened on occasion.

At the Turning Stone Resort in Verona (between Syracuse and Utica), that's a challenge. The resort, operated by the Oneida Indian Nation, has more than a dozen different bars (and even more restaurants). Each has its own cocktail list.

So Turning Stone's beverage and nightlife staff created a "cocktail test kitchen" to bring some order to the process. "As cocktails evolve, we can't be too slow to change," said Jerry Marrello, the resort's nightlife and beverage director. "We have to be forward-thinking."

The cocktail test kitchen started in 2015, in a small space tucked behind the Turquoise Tiger, Turning Stone's cocktail lounge and live music room "inspired by 1940s film noir." It looks more like a kitchen than a bar. It's got storage shelves and a big refrigerator for ingredients, stainless-steel counters and a sink. It's loaded with lemons, cocktail bitters, milk, juices and, of course, a roster of gins, bourbons, vodkas and rums.

Jeff Hannagan of the Turning Stone Resort Casino in Verona makes a Romancing the Stone cocktail in the resort's "cocktail test kitchen." *Author's photo.*

"It's a safe haven for us," Marrello said. "It's a safe little nook for us to play around and experiment."

The players—they call themselves the beverage committee—include Marrello, nightlife manager Vinny Belfiore and Jeff Hannagan, assistant manager for bar operations. They'll also round up others, for instance, the chefs or bar staff at the particular venue whose list they're working on.

"We also raid the chefs' kitchens if there's something there we want to use," Hannagan said. "That's the fun of it—sometimes you just change one little thing and you've got a whole new drink."

One of the first drinks to come of the test area was Romancing the Stone, a signature drink for the entire resort. It's a berry bomb, made with blueberry vodka, fresh blueberries and Chambord, a raspberry liqueur, topped with champagne.

The team is constantly looking for cocktail trends. Tea-infused cocktails heated up and so, in a way, did deep cold ones, made with dry ice that can chill a drink down to -25 degrees. Yet the cocktail test kitchen committee is also aware that serving the customers' desires is key.

"A lot of people are comfortable with certain things, like vodka and cranberry or rum and coke," Belfiore said. "It takes time and patience to convince them to try something new. It's a challenge that our bartenders are up for. They say, 'Try this, it's really good.'"

Once a new drink or drinks list is developed, it goes out to the venues in the resort. Customers then provide feedback that the cocktail staff listens to. Behind the bar, it's up to the bartender to sell the drinks—and that often comes with a bit of flair or entertainment.

"Everything we do has to have some kind of entertainment," Marrello said. "Showmanship and flair in mixing drinks is just as important in a bar as having good conversation."

These are some of the drinks devised at the Turning Stone cocktail test kitchen and now served at the resort.

Romancing the Stone
From Turning Stone Resort Casino

½ ounce Chambord
8 to 10 blueberries
½ ounce lemon juice
1 ½ ounces Stoli Blueberry Vodka
¼ ounce egg whites

Champagne to top
Lemon twist, for garnish

Muddle Chambord, blueberries and lemon juice in shaker glass. Add ice, vodka and egg whites. Shake until cold and frothy, double strain into champagne flute. Top with champagne and lemon twist garnish.

Fifth Street Fizz
From Turning Stone Resort Casino

1 ounce Plymouth Sloe Gin
¾ ounce Campari
Dash bitters
Pink grapefruit puree, to taste
½ ounce lemon juice
1 ounce simple syrup
Champagne
Lemon twist, for garnish

Combine all ingredients except champagne and lemon in shaker tin, shake until cold. Strain into champagne flute, top with champagne and garnish.

DISCO LEMONADE: THE COCKTAIL IN A CAN

Ben Reilley may seem just like a guy who runs a distillery. In reality, he's something of a drinks pioneer.

In 2016, his two-year-old Life of Reilley Distilling & Wine Company in Madison County, just east of Syracuse, launched a product called Disco Lemonade. It was the first "cocktail in a can" made from hard spirits produced in New York State and one of the first in the United States.

It's a whole new chapter in the long history of the American mixed drink, and a twenty-first-century example of Upstate New York ingenuity in spirits and cocktails.

Reilley's Disco Lemonade is a blend made from his distillery's raspberry vodka, plus lemonade and mint. When the vodka (40 percent alcohol) is mixed with the lemonade, it comes out at 6.5 percent alcohol, about the same as many India Pale Ales and a little stronger than most domestic premium beers like Bud or Coors. It's a pale yellow color, much like homemade lemonade.

But why put it in cans?

"We live in a place where people have boats, go to the beach or the park and so on," said Reilley, whose distillery is on Route 20 near the village of Cazenovia, in the heart of New York State. "Cans are much more practical, easier to carry. And that fits in with that carefree lifestyle."

Disco Lemonade, as a cocktail, had been around for several years, usually made with vodka, blue curaçao and lemonade. And the drinks industry had been awash for a couple of decades with flavored malt beverages like Smirnoff Ice or Mike's Hard Lemonade (which have a fermented beer-like base). Those are typically sold in bottles and cans.

But in 2014, Reilley had the idea to put a version of Disco Lemonade in cans using his own distilled spirits as the base. He saw it as a way to market his vodka to a wider audience and build an identity for his distillery. (Life of Reilley also makes a premium unflavored vodka and a vanilla vodka.)

The inspiration, he said, came when he and his wife, Siobhan, were at a summer bonfire party and noticed how many people came in carrying six-packs of Bud Light Lime-A-Rita (a beer-based flavored beverage made by brewing giant Anheuser-Busch InBev). So they set out on a mission: create something that would be a true cocktail, using hard spirits, not beer, that would work well in cans. The formula that clicked has Life of Reilley raspberry vodka, fresh-squeezed lemonade and an infusion of mint leaves.

"It's really not that sweet," Reilley said, "and that shot of mint in the aroma really kicks it up."

But we're a little ahead of the story, because it took a while before Disco Lemonade in cans could get to market. It had to be approved for sale by state and federal regulators. The novelty of the product meant that federal and state alcohol regulators weren't sure how to handle it. They kept comparing it to those beer-based malt products like Mike's Hard Lemonade or Smirnoff Ice.

But the use of a distilled spirit—in this case vodka—put Disco Lemonade in a different legal category. "We had a lot of conversations back and forth about that with the TTB [the federal agency that regulates alcohol]," Reilley said. "Eventually we got it sorted out."

Clearing the legal hurdles did come with one stipulation for Disco Lemonade: since it is a distilled spirit beverage, it cannot be sold in grocery stores or convenience markets, which is where you'll find beer in New York. It must be sold in liquor stores, along with other hard spirits and wine.

But that, Reilley believes, works to his advantage. He doesn't compete side-by-side with beer. Liquor stores have welcomed his product, because it gives them something to sell that customers come back in for more frequently than, say, vodka or whiskey.

"They like that 'turn and burn' that you get with this," Reilley said. "Customers might be back every week to stock up on Disco."

With Disco Lemonade, Reilley found, he could carve his own special niche in the surging distilled spirits business.

"It's the only product I've seen that skews 50/50 with men and women," Reilley said. "It's going to be what we're known for, I think. I think this category is coming on and it's here to stay."

KEGWORKS: BUILDING A BAR ONLINE

Mixing a good cocktail these days is no longer just for professional bartenders. No one knows that more than David Rivers, proprietor of a worldwide drinks business that has its base in the Buffalo suburbs. He launched an online retail business called Kegworks in 1998 and, in 2016, spun off an affiliate called Behind the Bar (behindthebar.com).

Kegworks at first specialized in the things a dedicated beer drinker might need, including glassware, bar mats and the kegerator (a small refrigerator specially outfitted to hold and dispense beer from a keg). The company moved into bar tools, tap systems, cocktail ingredients and all the necessities to set up your own "man cave," including signs.

Kegworks' customers have always included both bar professionals and the home mixologist, but the breakdown is hard to pinpoint because, after all, it's an online business serving domestic and international customers. Rivers thinks it might be a 50/50 split.

Tracking his business put Rivers in the perfect spot to witness the resurgence of interest in the cocktail. While the cocktail categories—tools, glassware and such—have "grown exponentially" in recent years, he said, it's the cocktail ingredient side that has provided the biggest boom.

His inventory of bitters, syrups, mixers, garnishes and more grew as more people discovered "the joy of mixology" (not coincidentally, the name of a cocktail guide by Gary Regan). Imagine Rivers's joy when he discovered that

Fee Brothers, a supplier of many of those ingredients, was located in nearby Rochester. "I got in my car and drove there in the middle of a snowstorm. We were the first to put their stuff online."

The search for vintage ingredients for classic cocktail continues to drive much of the business, Rivers said. "It's really those specialty, hard-to-find things—someone may read about a certain item and then look for it and discover we have it."

Although he split the beer side and cocktail side of his business into separate (but linked) sites in 2016, Rivers sees them as parallel.

"The whole craft cocktail industry is mirroring the craft beer industry," he said. "I'm happy to see the stock of both ticking up."

AN UPSTATE EYE-OPENER

For me, writing this book was an eye-opener. I uncovered the history and lore of spirits and cocktails in Upstate New York and made my introduction to the modern revival of both.

In that spirit, I'll leave you with a real Upstate eye-opener: the New York State Fair Bloody Mary, which highlights some of the iconic flavors of Upstate New York. It was introduced to the fair in 2016 by Ben Eberhardt and the Hospitality Concepts company of Hamilton, who run the Fair's Empire Room. (They're the same people who gave us the modern Flaming Rum Punch at the Gould Hotel in Seneca Falls.)

As you'll see, this drink, like many of the best stories and legends of Upstate drinks history, is all about the garnish.

The New York State Fair Bloody Mary
From the Empire Room at the New York State Fair, Syracuse

1½ ounces 1911 Established Vodka
Bloody Mary mix
1 Buffalo chicken wing
1 grape tomato
1 boiled shrimp
1 slice of Italian sausage (such as Gianelli)
1 salt potato

A History

1 slice of cheddar cheese
State Fair spiedie sauce
Lime wedge
2 olives
Celery stalk

Fill glass with ice. Pour in vodka and Bloody Mary mix. Place next six ingredients on a skewer and drizzle with spiedie sauce. Put lime wedge and two olives on a toothpick. Lay skewer and toothpick over the glass and add celery stalk.

BIBLIOGRAPHY

Abbott, Patrick J. "Native American and Alaskan Native Aboriginal Use of Alcohol." Centers for American Indian and Alaska Native Health, Colorado School of Public Health/University of Colorado Denver.

Andreatta, David. "Remember the Harvey Wallbanger?" *Rochester Democrat & Chronicle*, October 24, 2016.

Andrist, Ralph K. *The Erie Canal*. Rockville, MD: American Heritage, 2016.

Asbury, Herbert. "Professor Jerry Thomas." *American Mercury*, December 1927.

Balcom, Lawrence. "Junior Bootleggers." Traditional Arts in Upstate New York. http://northcountryfolklore.org/river_stories/clayton.html.

Barnes, Steve. "Toast to the Travers Revealed." *Albany Times-Union*, August 16, 2008.

Beebe, Lucius. *The Stork Club Bar Book*. Greensboro, NC: New Day Publishing, 2003.

Bond, Nancy. "Prohibition—Depression—Bootlegging." November 13, 2014. thousandislandslife.com.

"Bottoms Up! A History of the Brewing Industry in Syracuse." Pamphlet No. 12 in the Portraits of the Past series, Onondaga Historical Association, Syracuse, New York, 1997.

Bouchard, J. William, Justin DiVirgilio, Kevin Moody and Walter Wheeler et al. "Beyond the North Gate: Archeology on the Outskirts of Colonial Albany." Hartgen Archeological Associates Inc. Rensselaer, New York, October 2005.

Brown, Phil. "The Legacy of the Jewish Catskills." New York State Archives, 2011.

Bullock, Tom. *The Ideal Bartender* (1917). Reprint titled *173 Pre-Prohibition Cocktails*. Jenks, OK: Howling at the Moon Press, 2001.

Caiafa, Frank. *The Waldorf-Astoria Bar Book*, Rev. ed. New York: Penguin Books, 2016.

Cazentre, Don. "Cocktail History Happened in Upstate New York." *Post-Standard*, July 28, 2009.

———. "Disco Lemonade: Upstate NY's First Cocktail in a Can, Finally Ready for Its Debut." July 12, 2017. NYup.com.

———. "Turning Stone's Cocktail Test kitchen: Where New Drinks Are Stirred, Shaken and Sampled." June 7, 2016. NYup.com.

——. "Wine, Whiskey and Women." *The Good Life*, May 1, 2014.

Cooper, James Fenimore. *The Spy*, 1821. From *The Complete Works of James Fenimore Cooper*. Delphi Classics, 2013.

Crockett, A.S. *The Old Waldorf-Astoria Bar Book* (1934). Greensboro, NC: New Day Publishing, 2003.

Croswell, Harry, et. al. *Balance & Columbian Repository* (Hudson, New York). May 6 and May 13, 1806.

Curtis, Wayne. *And a Bottle of Rum: A History of the New World in Ten Cocktails*. New York: Three Rivers Press, 2006.

D'Imperio, Chuck. *A Taste of Upstate New York*. Syracuse, NY: Syracuse University Press, 2015.

Dionese, Christine. "Rochester Cocktail Revival." *Edible Finger Lakes*, May 1, 2015.

Felten, Eric. *How's Your Drink? Cocktails, Culture and the Art of Drinking Well*. Chicago: Surrey Books, 2007.

Grimes, William. "The Bartender Who Started It All." *New York Times*, October 31, 2007.

———. "On Language: Through a Cocktail Glass, Darkly." *New York Times Magazine*, August 25, 1991.

———. *Straight Up or On the Rocks: The Story of the American Cocktail*. New York: North Point Press, 2001.

Haara, Brian. "False Advertising and the Legacy of Duffy's Pure Malt Whiskey." Sipp'n Corn. Last modified January 8, 2014. sippncorn. blogspot.com/2014/01/false-advertising-and-legacy-of-duffys.html.

Haigh, Ted. "The Origin of the Cocktail." *Imbibe*. February 24, 2009. http://imbibemagazine.com/origin-of-the-cocktail.

————. *Vintage Spirits and Forgotten Cocktails (Deluxe Edition)*. Beverly, MA: Quarry Books, 2009.

Hess, Robert. "A Tribute to Jerry Thomas." Drink Boy. April 5, 2003. http://www.drinkboy.com/Articles/Article.aspx?itemid=23.

Jablonski, Peter. "History of the Whiskey Business in Buffalo." http://buffaloah.com/h/whiskey.

Kelly, Jack. *Heaven's Ditch: God, Gold and Murder on the Erie Canal*. New York: St. Martin's Press, 2016

McDonough, Patsy. *McDonough's Bar-Keepers Guide and Gentlemen's Sideboard Companion*. Rochester, NY: 1883.

McEneny, John J. *Albany: Capital City on the Hudson*. Sun Valley, CA.: American Historical Press, 1998.

Mencken, Henry L. *The American Language*. New York: Knopf, 1937.

New York Times. "A Noted Saloon Keeper Dead." December 16, 1885.

Niagara County Historical Society. "Bicentennial Moments: The First Cocktail." http://www.niagara2008.com/history99.html.

Powell, Stephen R. *Rushing the Growler: A History of Brewing in Buffalo*. Buffalo, NY: Apogee Productions, 1996.

Reddicliffe, Steve, and Christopher Buckley. *The Essential New York Times Book of Cocktails*. Kennebunkport, ME: Cider Mill Press, 2015.

Regan, Gary. *The Joy of Mixology*. New York: Clarkson Potter, 2003.

Regan, Gary, and Mardee Haidin Regan. "The History of Spirits in America." Distilled Spirits Council. http://www.discus.org/heritage/spirits.

Scientific Bar Keeping: A Collection of Recipes and New Fancy Mixed Drinks. Buffalo, NY: E.N. Cook & Co. Distillers, 1884.

Simonson, Robert. "A Regional Oddball, Resurrected for Chilliest of Days." In *The Essential New York Times Book of Cocktails*. Kennebunkport, ME: Cider Mill Press, 2015.

————. "Searching for Harvey Wallbanger," *Saveur*, December 14, 2012.

Sullivan, Jack. "Buffalo's Gustav Was the Other Fleischmann Brother." Those Pre-Prohibition Whiskey men! Last modified July 6, 2012. http://pre-prowhiskeymen.blogspot.com/2012/07/buffalos-gustav-was-other-fleischmann.html.

————. "Charles Tracey: Mixing Politics with Whiskey." Those Pre-Prohibition Whiskey Men! Last modified July 23, 2011. http://pre-prowhiskeymen.blogspot.com/2011/07/charles-tracey-mixing-politics-with.html.

―――. "How Mr. Duffy Outwitted Uncle Sam." Those Pre-Prohibition Whiskey Men! Last modified May 31 2011. http://pre-prowhiskeymen.blogspot.com/2011/05/how-mr-duffy-outwitted-uncle-sam.html.

Syracuse Post-Standard. "The Mamie Taylor." March 7, 1902.

Thomas, Jerry. *The Bar-Tender's Guide.* New York: Dick & Fitzgerald, 1887.

―――. *How to Mix Drinks* (1862). Kansas City, MO: Andrews McMeel Publishing, 2013.

Tulloch, Katrina. "Rochester Cocktail Revival Celebrates Centuries of Boozy Decadence." May 9, 2016. NYup.com.

Winship, Kihm. "Skaneateles Whiskey." Skaneateles: The Character and Characters of a Lakeside Village. Last modified March 11, 2011. kihm6.wordpress.com/2011/03/01/skaneateles-whiskey, March 2011.

Wondrich, David. "Ancient Mystery Revealed! The Real History (Maybe) of How the Cocktail Got Its Name." *Saveur,* January 14, 2016.

―――. "How to Make a Stone Fence." *Esquire,* November 6, 2007.

―――. *Imbibe! From Absinthe Cocktail to Whiskey Smash, a Salute in Stories and Drinks to "Professor" Jerry Thomas, Pioneer of the American Bar.* New York: The Penguin Group (Perigree), 2007.

INDEX

ABOUT THE AUTHOR

Don Cazentre is a veteran journalist who has been writing about beer and the alcoholic beverage industry since the mid-1990s. He is the craft beer, wine and spirits writer for NYup.com and the coauthor of *New York Breweries* (2nd ed.). He lives in Syracuse, New York.